UNDERSTANDING AUTISM

Useful Information for Dealing with Autism
from Parents who Have Lived with it 24/7
with Four Children in the Autistic Spectrum

UNDERSTANDING AUTISM

Useful Information for Dealing with Autism
from Parents who Have Lived with it 24/7
with Four Children in the Autistic Spectrum

by
Lori Rakieski
with ## Robert S. Nahas

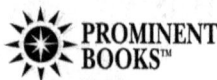

Written by:	Lori Rakieski with Robert S. Nahas
Cover Design:	Writer Services, LLC ™
Editing & Proofreading:	Loral A. Nahas - www.writerservices.net
Book Design & Typeset:	Writer Services, LLC ™

10 Digit ISBN 0-9800705-3-8

13 Digit ISBN 978-0-9800705-3-8

1. Parents of Autistic Children: Self-help, Self-Growth, Motivational, Experiences

Published by:

PROMINENT BOOKS™

Printed and bound in the U.S.A.

Prominent Books and the sunburst compass logo are Trademarks of Prominent Books, LLC

Table of Contents

THIS BOOK'S CONVENTIONS   1

INTRODUCTION   3

CHAPTER 1: ABOUT AUTISM   15

CHAPTER 2: DEALING WITH AUTISM   21

CHAPTER 3: HANDLING THE STRESS   30

CHAPTER 4: GETTING IN CONTROL   40

CHAPTER 5: ASSISTANCE FOR CHILD AND
FAMILY   51

CHAPTER 6: HOW TO GET ASSISTANCE   61

CHAPTER 7: EDUCATION AND THERAPY   78

CHAPTER 8: SENSORY INTEGRATION   100

CHAPTER 9: SAFETY & SECURITY MEASURES   118

CHAPTER 10: OTHER CHALLENGES   132

CHAPTER 11: A BETTER UNDERSTANDING FOR
ALL   147

CHAPTER 12: WHAT AUTISM HAS TAUGHT ME 156

BIOGRAPHY   **165**

RECOMMENDED READING   **166**

❧ ACKNOWLEDGEMENTS ❧

I would like to thank my mother and father, Rick and Carol Wuenschell, Mary and John Schoemer, Rick and Angela Wuenschell, Ken and RoseMary Wuenschell, Judy and Matthew Herbstritt, the Young family and all of my co-workers at Elk Regional Health Center for their continuous support and love.

I dedicate this book to my loving, supportive husband Daniel and our beautiful children: Mitchell, Alexander, Danielle, Adam, Erik, Lauren and Dean, and to autistic children and their parents everywhere.

--Lori Rakieski

Very special thanks go to Robert S. Nahas for his writing and editorial input with this written work. His literary knowledge, expertise and input was invaluable to the overall project, and his kindness and understanding has been greatly appreciated.

৪৩

This Book's Conventions

This book is pretty straight forward in its delivery of information. But just to clarify a few minor details:

Using of Gender

In the name of saving grammar from the erosion of improper use, when referring to a non-specific individual, random gender of the pronoun (he or she) is used in this book. For instance, when referring to a specialist, in general, either "he" or "she" will be used without bias to refer to both genders.

You will be spared from the overuse of "repetitive clutter" of "he/she" as well as staying clear of the improper use of the word "they" in these circumstances. ("They" is only supposed to be used when referring to more than one person, place or thing.)

When Referring to Parents, Guardians, Caretakers...

In the same spirit of a clutter-free book, it is fully acknowledged here that there are a number of individuals who might have custody in the care of a child. Therefore, we use "parent" to refer to anyone (parent, parents, guardian, caretaker...) who may be caring for the child.

Introduction

Proud Parents

The birth of a child is miraculous, and the experience breathtaking. If you've been there, you know what I mean. If you're expecting your first child, you have much to look forward to in this experience.

The typical fears that haunt parents during the carrying months of whether their child will be healthy, normal and perfect in every way are innate to the process. First observations peer to see that everything is in the right place and the fingers and toes contain sets of five. Perfect!

The initial gasp of earthly air and the release of that first cry conclude that all is well. And the worry that rested at the back of one's lobes for the past nine months quickly dissipate into sheer excitement.

A mother giving birth longs to finally hold and make contact with the child she has carried under her heart for nine months. This feeling of anticipation is difficult to describe as life cannot be compared with physical possessions for analogies.

My Mitchell was born September 8, 1997. He was my firstborn. I remember crying and thinking to myself, thank God for my son, as I held him in my arms. Dan, my husband, wrapped him tightly in a blanket and took him out of the room to meet his new grandparents who were eagerly waiting outside the door.

After a short while Dan brought him back in, laid him in my arms and bragged how our new son, Mitchell Dennis Rakieski, was going to be a star quarterback. Football, you see, is my husband's favorite sport and he had always dreamed of playing this sport with his sons. He often joked about our son playing for the Steelers – his favorite team.

I was so happy to be a mother. This was all I wanted in life. I often said if I had to fail everything in life but be told I was a good mother, then I accomplished all I ever wanted.

My husband is a very sweet, loving, patient man who wanted a large family just like me. We planned on this since the early days of our relationship and living happily ever after.

Mitchell achieved all of the milestones of a typical child. He rolled over at four months, sat up at six months, crawled at nine months and walked at fourteen months. He babbled a lot as a baby and a toddler. This babbling and not talking recognizable words would be the first sign something was wrong.

My Alex was born October 31, 1998. He was my birthday present. I found out I was pregnant with him on my 28th birthday, February 26, 1998. Mitchell was only five months old. I called Dan at work to give him the news, "You are going to be a father again!" He yelled and screamed to his co-workers, "I am going to be a dad again!" "Didn't your wife just have a baby?" they asked. It didn't matter. Our dream for a big family was coming true.

When our second son, Alexander Richard, was born, I felt proud and happier than I have ever been in my life. I realized that I finally had a wonderful husband

and an excellent beginning to a large family.

When Alex was born no one made it to the hospital in time; he was born so quickly. It was Halloween at 3:30 in the afternoon. Dan was finally able to contact my parents. My mom was shopping at JC Penney and was paged to come to the phone where she was told (by my future sister-in-law) she was going to be a grandmother again. My dad was rabbit hunting.

Everyone did eventually arrive at the hospital, including my dad who came with two mum plants – two plants for two kids. My mom came to the hospital with Mitchell. He was crawling around the room. Then when my mother held him up to see his new brother, Mitchell looked at him and said "kitty." This was a word Mitchell had just learned.

Alex, like Mitchell, achieved all the milestones of any typical child. He rolled over at four months, sat up at five months, crawled at five months and walked at fourteen months but he said very few words. It was at twenty months that these few words stopped altogether and when I came to gravely suspect something might be wrong.

Still unaware of the circumstances with Mitchell and Alex, I was flying higher than a kite being the mother of two beautiful children and the wife of a loving husband. All seemed perfect and well on the way to having a big happy family.

When Alex was one year old and Mitchell two years old, we decided to try for another baby. It was October 11, 1999 that I found out I was pregnant again. Dan and I were elated. It was at this time that we stumbled upon a house in St. Marys, PA.

The house was old but very spacious, just perfect for a big family to live in. A five bedroom house with a backyard made things that much more exciting as we continued to move toward our familial goal. The neighbors even had four children right around the boys' age.

At the bottom of my heart I hoped deeply for a little girl. Another boy, of course, would have been just fine with me. But a girl to be close to simply because of the connection between females – similar to the unique bond that had grown between Dan and the boys out of sheer masculinity – would have been wonderful.

My little girl, Danielle, was born on June 27, 2000. She came three days past her due date and was my biggest baby thus far – eight pounds, thirteen ounces. In the delivery room Dan looked at her and said, "My beautiful baby girl." She had short black hair with a very round face – she was perfect! I couldn't wait for her brothers to meet her.

Danielle was a very quiet, easygoing baby. She rarely cried but did babble, say some words but her vocabulary did not advance past "baby-talk." She, too, achieved the milestones of a typical young child – rolling over at 4 months, sitting up at 5 and walking at 10 months. She would follow her older brothers around the house eagerly wanting to join them in play. Danielle always had a smile on her face. But at around 18 months of age, Dan and I noticed a change in her personality. The change was so dramatic and noticeable that we feared something might be wrong.

Back in May of 2000, about one month before Danielle was born, I had taken Mitchell and Alex to the pediatrician for check-ups. It was at this time that the doctor felt Mitchell's language should have been more discernable and recommended he see a speech therapist. Being eight months pregnant, I felt Mitchell could wait until after I had the baby to see a therapist. Mitchell was 2 ½ years old and was babbling like a baby. I was concerned at what the doctor had said, but not alarmed.

After Danielle was born I contacted the Early Intervention office. It was now July. They sent someone out to the house to evaluate Mitchell. The service coordinator had decided that since Mitchell would be three years old in a couple of months, it would be more beneficial for him to move on to the age three special education preschool. (Early Intervention only works with children from birth to three years of age).

The paperwork was enormous and very tedious. But on September 19, 2000, Mitchell started preschool as recommended. My plan was for him to attend this school for one year and then take him to a regular Catholic preschool in town after that. He needed help with his speech, so I thought.

At about this time, Alex's incidence of talking had dropped significantly to the point of being almost non-extant. He would go days without saying a word. He also began to bang his head against the wall and floor out of frustration when he couldn't get across what he wanted. He would freefall down the stairs and climb the bookcases in our living room. I remember saying to Dan that this was not right and that something was wrong with Alex. "Alex is just active" my family would say. I sensed there was more but I couldn't figure out what it was.

As the months rolled by I noticed a significant difference in Mitchell's speech. He was finally saying some sentences, repeating words, pointing to objects and saying what they were. I was very happy with his progress. At the same time, I was bewildered why he could not answer a question or carry on a conversation. I would ask him, "What did you do in school today?" yet he would not acknowledge the questions at all. I also noticed this in Alex as well, and Alex would give very little eye contact. Sometimes it seemed as though he were deaf. This worried me a great deal but since it was happening to both of them, I thought it was a normal part of the developing process.

Danielle at this time was rolling over, looking at me and smiling while babbling baby talk. She would watch whomever entered and exited the room and showed that she was aware of her surroundings.

Not long into Mitchell's term, the special education preschool called me and asked if Dan and I would meet with them. We were told that Mitchell was not participating with the other children. It seemed he did not know what to do with toys. He would throw them or hold them up and let them drop to the floor. His teacher and therapist noticed very little imaginative or purposeful play. They also were concerned about his poor eye contact and how he would spin in circles if there was a change in the routine of the classroom.

They told Dan and I that they would like to have a psychologist come in and give them some ideas of how to get Mitchell to participate in school better. Dan and I agreed to the psychologist's consultation.

Being that Dan and I only thought Mitchell had poor speech skills and that his behavior in the classroom was connected in some way with this, the situation didn't seem too alarming or serious to us. But little did we know that the school was consulting a professional over greater concerns – to confirm their theories as to why Mitchell had been exhibiting so many different behaviors. We were not made privy to their considerations in our meeting with the preschool. So we left simply thinking our Mitchell had poor speech skills. Oh how I wish it would have been that simple.

The psychologist visited the school and observed Mitchell on February 8, 2001. She called me that afternoon asking if she could come over the next day at 1:30pm. February 9th would become a major turning point in my life. It would change me forever.

Getting the News

When the psychologist arrived, Mitchell, Alex and Danielle were all napping. The house was quiet. She proceeded to tell Dan and I how the visit went at school.

She spoke very slowly, sort of hedging, and I could tell she had more to say than what she was disclosing. She said that she noticed Mitchell sitting alone most of the time and commented how poor his eye contact was. Then, all at once she looked straight into my eyes and asked, "Have you ever heard of autism?" I answered "Yes." She then blurted out, "Well I think Mitchell has this."

I was shocked and felt warm tears quickly well in my eyes. She then proceeded to read off a long list of characteristics of autism. I watched her through my warped vision as I tried to keep my tear-filled eyes from letting go. I listened to her but absorbed very little of what she was saying. The word "autism" just stuck in my mind and I couldn't let go of it. Dan and I said nothing as she stood up and left our home. As the door closed behind the psychologist, Dan and I realized that the life we had (or thought we were creating) was gone at that moment.

It was time for Dan to leave for work. He looked at me in despair and walked out the door. As he left, the tears started falling. I cried and wailed out loud like I never had before in my life. I then looked up autism on the Internet and began reading. Between the falling tears I read all about this subject. As I read and sobbed, in through the door came Dan. He couldn't make it to work that day.

We held each other and cried. As we wept we both, at the same time, realized that this was probably what was wrong with Alex also.

We called our pediatrician and spoke with him about the possibility. He referred us to the Children's Hospital in Pittsburgh. It took four months to get an appointment but we needed to confirm, or annul, what we already knew in our hearts was the case.

The four months we waited for the appointment were painful. I could not eat, sleep or work. My heart was broken and the grief consumed me.

We brought Mitchell and Alex to the Children's Hospital in Pittsburgh, PA on 6-27-01 — this was Danielle's first birthday. They were both officially diagnosed with having autism on this date.

After Dan and I received the heartbreaking diagnosis of autism for our two beautiful boys, we wrestled with the thought of possibly not having anymore children. Dan and I cried bitterly at the thought of not fulfilling our dream, and I knew if I didn't have the children I so desired, I would always wonder what my life would have been like. We both expressed our wishes to have more children and our delight in being a parent and the joy we felt sharing our lives with our children. As parents of two autistic children already, we knew there was a risk that we could have other children with autism. This scary fact was examined that day and as I looked at my three beautiful, happy children in the back seat of the car, I couldn't help but feel unconditional love, pride and gratitude for their presence. How could I not want anymore children? The decision was final. Dan and I decided to bring other children into our family no matter what the risks.

On July 7, 2001, Dan and I were happy to get the news that I was pregnant. This was a nice surprise and I felt like God gave me a gift in the midst of all of our sadness and grief.

Adam Christopher Rakieski was born on March 2, 2002. When the nurse first gave him to me, I remember closing my eyes and thanking God for helping me make the decision to have more children. I also said a silent pray that possibly Adam would be spared from the silence that his brothers were facing. When I brought Adam home from the hospital, Mitchell, Alex and Danielle were sick with the flu. I sat up with the children at night and watched them sleep. The emotions I was feeling caught up with me and I wept. I held Adam and looked at my other three children and started thinking back to when they were babies. The thoughts were difficult to bear. Why would God hurt me like this? Why would he take away my dream? How can I do all that the children need me to do?

Six months after Mitchell and Alex were diagnosed, Dan and I saw some changes in our then 18 month old Danielle. She stopped talking and sunk into her own world. She would sit in front of the TV or at the table totally absorbed in what she was doing with absolutely no attention on her environment. Danielle would not respond to her name nor follow directions. She didn't like to be touched and would cry if I tried to hold her. My heart ached for her. Just six months earlier, she was not like this. What happened? Why did she change? The pain was unbearable. Dan and I watched Danielle disappear right before our eyes. Our smiling, friendly, outgoing baby changed into an expressionless, turned-in individual.

Danielle was diagnosed with PDD (Pervasive Developmental Disorder) on October 23, 2002. This is under the autism spectrum. She was eventually diagnosed with autism some months later.

As Adam grew I memorized everything I could about his childhood. I called his name and was relieved when he responded. I held him and smiled as he looked into my eyes and smiled. I watched him so closely. It was at this time that Danielle was diagnosed and I was emotionally numb from the news.

Adam had a lot of ear infections and eventually had to get tubes in his ears at 16 months of age. It was quickly after this that I noticed him not responding to his name and he was not developing any speech at all. I thought to myself, *it is just his ears*. I took him for hearing tests and to speech therapy. I would not let the possibility of autism enter into my head. Shortly before his second birthday, Adam was spinning things on the floor and watching them spin. He was flapping his hands and jumping up and down a lot. He then started climbing everything and not responding to his name at all. It was at this point I realized something was wrong. He started receiving occupational therapy, speech therapy, physical therapy and a special education teacher in the home. I watched Adam slowly fade away. The pain and sadness I felt was indescribable. I remember driving home from the store one day with Adam in the car. I stopped the car in a vacant parking lot. I got out of the car and open the door to the back seat. I sat in the back seat and cried. I looked at Adam and I said, "Please don't leave me for the world of autism. Please come back to me."

Adam was diagnosed with autism on December 13, 2004 at Children's Hospital in Pittsburgh. After I left the doctor's office and got onto the elevator that day, I stopped the elevator and cried. I looked down at Adam in the stroller and tearfully told him I was going to do everything I could to give him a good future. He smiled back at me as if he knew what I was saying. It was another sad day for Dan and Lori Rakieski and another piece of our hearts broken.

The children I thought I had were gone. I had to get to know my children all over again. Our dreams of what a parent should be and what our lives should be like were gone. We had to learn how to become parents all over again – parents of autistic children. We had to do things differently to help our children. The thoughts of seeing my children struggle with the simplest things was painful, but I knew that Dan and I were the only ones who would make things happen for these special children. It was all up to us. The responsibility was enormous, but this is what our children needed from us.

Living with Autism

The feeling of the pride and joy of having "perfect" children is what makes autism so horrific and heartbreaking to accept as a loving parent.

My name is Lori. I have three sons and a daughter with autism. Autism is a neurological disorder in clinical terms but according to a parent who experiences this on a daily basis, it is a monster that gradually changes your perfect child and the lives of those who love them forever.

I spent years searching for information to help myself and my husband, Dan, better manage as parents of such children. But we found no significant data, only moral support which we greatly appreciated.

But what was desperately needed was a book written by someone who had an autistic child themselves, not by a psychologist who studied about it in a classroom from text books. What was needed was an advisor who had lived day in, day out, 365 days-a-year with autism as part of their life. We greatly needed for others (teachers, people in the community, family…) to better understand autistic children in their needs as well as their abilities and not expect things that should not be expected. And we needed to be understood as to what we were going through as parents.

This book is going to enlighten, educate, interest, move, surprise and perhaps even disabuse you about children with autism. As a parent of four children within this spectrum, we are succeeding as I am sure all parents of autistic children do.

But I wish to share what I have learned from my beautiful children that no library, with its rows of books, could ever touch upon even faintly. I want to communicate what scientific data I have found through much research and trial and error. I want to offer up the unwritten, unspoken truth about what the parents and the other siblings go through; how ignorance causes unnecessary hardship. Most of all, I want to help my children, and all children with these challenges, by educating all who will listen so that their environments can become safe from needless injury or even death. And that they may be treated with more respect and understanding instead of invalidation and social abuse.

Whether you have an autistic child, work in the field of education or social services or just wish to better understand autism, this book will enlighten you with real-life information from a real-life family of four autistic children.

God Bless,
Lori Rakieski

ଧୀଠଷ

Chapter 1
About Autism

There are psychological textbook explanations that appropriately define autism and the autistic child but I have yet to find an adequate description that reveals the true essence of what an autistic child really is. This is because, I feel, it could only be properly described through the eyes of a loving parent.

Autism has many clinical definitions, but this word, according to a parent, means much more than a list of behavioral traits. My mission in this chapter is to best depict autism, not so much in its clinical list of traits, but by including the deeper, more personal reality of what autism is from a loving parent's intimate viewpoint.

Describing Autism

A parent's instinct is to protect their offspring and keep them at a safe distance from harm's way. Most would trade their lives in order to save one of their own without reservation. From a parent's perspective, watching autism slowly take over could be vaguely compared to someone kidnapping your child as you stand by watching through a looking glass without any ability to help save your child. But this horrid occurrence happens on a daily basis.

Autism is like a nightmare that you never wake up from. There is a pervasive feeling of overwhelm and helplessness because there's no immediate means of protecting your child from this invisible, insidious predator. It arrives without invitation and invades the family's constitution as it slowly steals your child away, right in front of you.

The child somehow becomes lost; their whole being changes. The desire to be held and make contact with the world wades. What makes it even harder is that, often, everything starts out perfectly. Bright, bubbly smiling balls of sunshine once bounced around our home. Out of nowhere, emotionless, daydream-like stares fixated upon nothing replace that exhilarated look of wonder about the world.

After my children were officially diagnosed with autism, my husband and I were devastated. An "apathetic helplessness" would best sum up the initial stage. After the initial shock, I felt a strong need to know all I could about autism. And though I didn't realize it at the time, this was the right thing to do.

I read book-after-book and learned, clinically, what this "thing" was that was taking over my beautiful children. I read definitions and learned of different strategies on how to modify and improve behaviors. It all seemed so overwhelming, but confronting it head on was the only way I was going to be able to do any good for my children.

It didn't take long for me to realize that autism was what I had been experiencing every day with my children. Their traits were textbook. I also realized that Dan and I were not alone in this tragedy. The statistics show that approximately 400,000 children are afflicted with autism. The instance of having two autistic children in the same family significantly drops and our circumstance of having four blood-related siblings with autism is astronomically rare.

The child, with all its qualities and personality once so familiar, goes away, seemingly overnight. What is left is a completely different individual. There is the same physical shape but the person inside seems not the same.

Unfortunately, a parent lives with autism daily and is reminded of the situation every second of every day. When Christmas comes around, I am reminded when I hear other parents complain about all the things their children have asked for on their Christmas lists to Santa. My children don't know how to play with toys. My children can't write lists or speak well enough to tell me what they want.

I sit them on Santa's lap and take them to church to see the baby Jesus, hoping they understand something about Christmas. They cannot tell me if they do.

I look out my window in the summer and see the neighborhood children playing baseball. I hear their laughs and wish my children could be part of their team. But my children have no desire to be that social and the other children do not welcome them into their circles.

Today, one in every 68 families has an autistic child in the United States, and this statistic is steadily increasing.

Different Worlds

When my children were first diagnosed I was determined *not* to let them sink into the autistic world. I wanted them with me. It is a difficult job but the child must be forced to stay in our world instead of sitting on the couch spinning truck wheels and blocking out everything in the environment. It is *vital* for the child to be involved in our world and learn how to tolerate it.

The more the child is kept with their attention in this world and allowed to visit the autistic world for brief moments daily (which the child needs), the greater chance the child will develop to their greatest potential.

Of course this does not happen overnight, but it is important to realize that everything done for the good of the child has positive results. The results may not be seen for days, months or years but *everything* counts. My Alex did not start saying words spontaneously until he was five years old. All of the sudden he could recall his colors, count to ten and name his shapes. Everything taught to him over the two-and-a-half years prior to this momentous event contributed to it even though I had been losing hope he would ever begin to talk.

They are Children First

The name "autism" to many people means something "bad" or "not normal." But underneath the word and diagnosis is a child. When dealing with all the "bad" parts of autism don't forget the child. Look at the goodness in your child and be thankful.

I look at Mitchell who really cares about people. If someone is sad or upset, he picks up on it and will come over with a hug or kiss. Mitchell loves Scooby Doo, swimming, reading and playing on the computer. Mitchell can read and write over one hundred words. He can count to one hundred and he loves school—my little bookworm.

Alex loves to fix things. If Dan is working on something, Alex is right beside him with his tool belt and play tools. He is sweet and gentle and has never hit or done anything aggressive to anyone. He loves to go fishing, help me cook and play on the computer.

Danielle loves her baby dolls. She pretends to feed them and tuck them in beside her at night. When she smiles she lights up a room. She especially loves the show Blues Clues. Danielle loves her bedroom and will play in it for hours.

Adam loves music. When he hears any kind of music he stops and smiles. He has found some interest in a musical keyboard that we purchased for him. Although he doesn't play a song per say, he plays the notes and puts his ear down to the keys to listen to the sounds. Adam also likes big hugs and will come to Dan and I for one quite often.

Sometimes I have to remind myself to look at them as young children, beyond the autism. I have to remember they are children first and foremost.

When my children were first diagnosed, I begged God to take my voice and reasoning skills and give them to Mitchell, Alex, Adam and Danielle. I asked for God to protect my precious autistic children from ridicule, shame and embarrassment. In a way I think that God knew that I had it in me all the time to give my children these gifts. I am their voice by writing this book and I am sharing their experiences to protect them from ridicule, shame and embarrassment.

౪০⍺

Chapter 2
Dealing with Autism

Dealing with autism usually begins with a few stages of emotions and reactions that must be traversed.

Denial

Initially, after it was suspected something was wrong with the children, Dan and I went through a denial stage. We asserted there was nothing wrong with our children. This phase for us lasted a very short time. As I read information on autism, I realized this was what was happening to my children. I remember reading some information late one night. As I read it all, I realized how much it was describing my children.

As I saw Danielle change, I realized what was happening to her. Especially when I saw my nephew, who is the same age as her, advance in receptive and expressive language and become so social.

As I witnessed Adam slowly change, I also knew what

was happening. Adam loved to play "peek-a-boo" and I remember playing this with him every chance I could. This is one of the games that autistic children cannot do. This game requires eye contact, some socialization and the ability to understand what was being said in order to respond back. When Adam stopped playing this game with me and began spinning objects on the floor, flapping his hands and not responding to his name, I knew the heartbreaking reality. My niece, who is the same age, was talking, responding, laughing and doing all she could for attention. I especially knew as I watched her progress and Adam become more and more distant.

Parents cannot be in denial for too long when it comes to autism. Every second an autistic child is not receiving therapy is a step backwards. But denial is a healthy reaction. It means you aren't simply willing to accept one or two opinions or prognosis—and you shouldn't. Important matters should always receive good research and validation. But this should move quickly once autism has been suggested or diagnosed.

Denial can't become non-confront. Instead, an adequate investigation into the subject from a variety of different sources should be made. This way, any reservations can be substantiated or annulled, and the truth can be known—whether your child actually is autistic, within the autistic spectrum or otherwise. Once you can feel confident of the circumstances, you can then make a decision and act on it.

When I did research on the Internet, books and whatever I could find on the subject, I looked at different perspectives (medical, alternative, etc.) too. If you're not convinced whether your child has autism or not, here's just a few places you can start with your research:

WEB SITES

Autistic Society of America
http://www.autism-society.org/

CDC: Autism Information Center
http://www.cdc.gov/ncbddd/dd/ddautism.htm

Autism Web
http://www.autismweb.com/

Center for the Study of Autism
www.autism.org

http://www.futurehorizons-autism.com/

BOOKS

The Autistic Spectrum: A Parent's Guide to Understanding and Treating Spectrum Disorders - Bryna Siegal

Autism: The Facts - Simon Baron-Cohen

Though denial *will* exist before an autism diagnosis becomes accepted, this denial should never interfere with the well-being of the child.

Acceptance

If you have found that your child has autism, accepting it can be difficult. But realize that facing the truth, whatever it is, is always the best policy. Nothing has ever improved on its own, in fact, in most cases things get worse when ignored.

That said, I think it is also important to get a second opinion from any professional(s) you see fit. With so many stories of misdiagnosing as well as questionable ailments these days, one cannot be too cautious.

Acceptance does not have to mean defeat under any circumstances. On the contrary, it opens the door to the possibility of overcoming the obstacle. Many great achievements have been made with autistic children in leading a normal, healthy lifestyle.

Grief

For the rearing parents, finding out that their child is afflicted with autism can bring up feelings of deep, indescribable grief. Some have described it as something similar to one dying in the family. This grieving process can be very overwhelming and the anguish does not go away quickly. But there are ways to rise above the negatives and turn things around to a more positive perspective.

As in any tragic event, the healing does come. How one approaches it will determine whether the healing will come quickly or be drawn out. As this is a subjective matter there are no simple guidelines to follow; each person must choose their own path in this healing process. But, again, dealing with it head on has been my saving grace.

Dealing with Autism

The grief that comes with autism is deeply seeded and always present, but there are ways to get through each day. One can turn a feeling of being "cheated out of the deal" to realizing that, perhaps, you were chosen because of your personal inner strength—a strength stronger than presently realized. Let's face it, most of us were never given a tensile strength test (a mechanical stress test given on different metals to see their breaking points) before this situation. In short, feeling regretful can move over to feeling more in control over the situation and not so much a victim of circumstance.

It is very difficult to see a child you love struggle and work so hard at everything. But on the other side of the coin, that child deserves a chance – the best chance possible. There is nothing more therapeutic, for both the parents and the child, than to DO something about it. Observing in anguish is being "in effect" of it. Grabbing it by the horns is being "in control." Parenting an autistic child is a full time job but it can be the most rewarding time of your life.

Adam got diagnosed close to Christmas. Dan and I decided that year not to go anywhere for the holidays and just stay home and enjoy our family. The sadness of having four autistic children, a life so different from everyone else's and a very difficult road ahead was the topic of our conversation over the holidays. Dan and I knew that the responsibility in making sure these children, and our other "typical children," are successful, happy and good individuals was going to be very rough road. I can remember crying in church on Christmas Day that year. I just pleaded for God to help us. "Here we go again." The grieving and sorrow just seemed to never go away.

Getting through the initial shock of an autism diagnosis takes time. In my case, I had four months prior to the initial diagnosis to come to terms with how my life and the lives of my family would change forever.

Give yourself time for the autism diagnosis to sink in. The day after a psychologist gave Dan and I the horrific news that our older sons might be autistic, we took the kids to the park. I remember, we just watched them run. We both had to accept the idea that there might actually be something wrong. The day after their official diagnosis in

June, we took the kids to Ocean City, Maryland. Dan and I needed to be with the kids and give ourselves a chance to grieve together. After Danielle was diagnosed in October we both took off work and took the kids to Pittsburgh for the weekend to visit my parents. We needed a chance to get through that initial shock.

Getting through the shock of autism *can* be accomplished. This does not mean the hurt will go away nor does it mean the pain will be forgotten, it simply means there are ways to push forward and muster up the hope that your child will be able to coexist in the world when older.

Dan and I decided not to tell a lot of people at first. We were both hurting and knew the more people that we told right away the more we would have to talk about it. I also knew that telling my family the children had autism would be painful and we would have had the extra burden of helping them through the grief as well. It was difficult for me to tell my parents because I knew I would be breaking their hearts just like mine was already broken. My parents were elated to be grandparents and they took pride in every one of their grandchildren. I knew the news would bring a lot of questions and worrying from my parents. I had to wait until the time was right for me to deal with all of this as well as my own grief.

Choosing the right time to tell others (family, close friends, co-workers) depends on the assumption of the predicted response from the recipients. It might seem obvious that the immediate family would be the first to be told but this may, or may not, be the best thing. Depending on what stage you are in should dictate who should be told, if anyone at all. The beginning stages require all of the strength one can bring just to make it through the day. Telling others who would break down over the news would not be a wise action to take. But if there are individuals – a special friend, aunt, uncle, priest – that you feel would be there for YOU, the moral support would, indeed, be advantageous to the healing process. The decision of when to tell the rest will be different for everyone but it must be at a time when you are willing to help them deal with it concurrently with your own healing process.

The same stages that you go through, will be gone through by them as well. They will be shocked. They will be in denial. They will feel anger and sadness. Therefore, you must be at a strong point, yourself, before you consider telling them.

The possible reactions from others are vast. Some of them might direct their denial right at you by claiming you are an unworthy parent while others might make covert insinuations of a similar kind. They might simply ask more questions than you're presently ready to deal with. The point here is not to make anyone wrong in how they react, as they are dealing with the situation the best way they are capable of. The greater point here is to protect yourself from any unnecessary anguish that might compound things and slow your own healing process. Once again, it is the child that needs strong parents helping them out as soon as possible.

Dan's parents knew first. They did not talk about it much at all. This surprised me. His mother wanted us to announce it to the rest of the family. We just simply couldn't do this. The pain was too deep and we knew the rest of the family would have many questions that Dan and I at the time did not want to answer.

Eventually, the entire family was told, but it was done at a time when the autism could be explained by us with an open mind.

I find myself very angry at times – at God, my husband and myself. Sometimes I can't even find a good reason why. There is a fine line between anger and love. It is because I love my children so much that I get so angry. It's the continuous pain of watching all that they must endure in their lives that angers me so. Not understanding what they want to say to me and seeing them not duplicate what I say to them is very difficult to endure.

The autistic child demands so much patience and time that it can become overwhelming. For me, expressing anger once in a while works. I can remember being so mad one time coming home from the grocery store that I just yelled out "God! Can't you give me one more day of a normal life?" Why did you take my normal life away?!"

Releasing one's anger is a good way to relieve some of the emotion and tension that builds up day after day in dealing with autism. Others might find a good crying would do the job.

Whatever the means, this release must not compound things by using others as targets. Lashing out at your spouse, family, friends – the people that mean the most to you – can only cause more pain that does not need to be there to compound things in your life.

Whatever way you find that works, no matter what your position is (parent, teacher, therapist, etc.), it is good to release some steam but ONLY when the child is not around and cannot hear you.

I also remind myself that no matter how hard autism is to deal with for me, it is still so much more difficult for my children.

I can remember being so far into despair that I found it difficult to go to work in the morning. I couldn't bear to hear others speak about their children. The depression was so substantial. I didn't know how I was going to get through it. Then one day at work a young girl came up to me and told me about her autistic brother. She said to me "God only gives special children to special people who he knows is going to take care of them." This stuck with me. I began to wonder whether God had big plans for my children and knew that I would take care of them and help them to be successful at his plan. I then realized that being angry at God helped get the emotions out, but having some faith and trust in him makes the grief seem more tolerable. I then started using prayer as a means of getting out my anger, emotions, fears and deep despair. I wanted God to help me understand. Prayer became a strong part of getting through each day and being able to face the hard core of grief.

As mentioned in other words at the beginning of this chapter, confronting something unpleasant opens the door to solving problems. When I was depressed, I didn't resort to medication or remain in denial. The only way out of a problem is right through the front door.

ಐಡಿ

Chapter 3
Handling the Stress

A child is a connection between two individuals who love each other. When a child is diagnosed with a serious condition like autism, the parents are left to deal with their own personal sorrow and grief as well as consoling their partner. Stress develops between the two parents because of the many deep feelings each is experiencing and dealing with, the daily challenges of having an autistic child, the need to understand what autism is and finding a way to console and support each other in their time of despair. It is difficult for a marriage to survive under such intense circumstances.

The word, "stress," means many things to many different people. Some define stress as working too many long hours at the office while others see it as being home all day with their children. Everyone tolerates stress differently and everyone reacts to it in different ways. For me, stress is getting through the busy schedule the children have while working outside the home, cleaning the house, writing bills, dealing with the daily, specific challenges the children have and effectively communicating with all the individuals who work with my children daily. Some days the pressure and expectations of being a good mother, loving wife and supporting co-worker are overwhelming. The bottom line is a family with autism has great needs.

I feel torn between home and work at times. But Dan and I have found ways to get through the pressure, making days less stressful and more enjoyable. My mission of this chapter is to share my strategies for getting through each demanding day. I use these techniques every day and I find myself less stressed and much calmer.

1. **Dissect each day and make a list of assignments.** I look at my calendar each morning to see what needs done for that day and the next day. I then look at each appointment, each scheduled time my child needs to be somewhere, each scheduled time my husband and I need to be somewhere and I write down a list of what needs to be accomplished in order for us or our children to be where we need to be.

   For instance; on Monday morning at 8:00am Alex has therapy at the nearby hospital. Dan and I make sure that Alex has transportation there and home. We make sure we write down any questions we have for the therapists or comments that they need to know. Around this therapy schedule, Dan and I plan who is going to go with the Alex to therapy (sometimes the TSS worker, his case manager or advocate goes with him) also.

   This is one example of the many things to do for the entire day. By dissecting the day into each task and making sure we write each one down, it puts order and a sense of being in control instead of overwhelmed.

Any phone calls that need to be made and what other individuals working with the kids might need to know about therapy that day are written down. For instance; the teacher at the special education preschool might need to know about a sensory technique the sensory integration therapists found valuable in outpatient therapy. By dissecting each day, I am less likely to forget to do something and I am more focused on accomplishments. It makes me feel good to know I got something done. And this is more noticeable when you can actually see them checked off on the page.

By dissecting one day at a time I find the busy, tight schedule to be much more tolerable and I am less likely to become overwhelmed and stressed.

2. **Schedule appointments or therapy sessions efficiently.**

Dan and I try to minimize craziness by scheduling appointments or therapy sessions consecutively or by limiting the scheduling to one per day. For instance, Alex and Danielle both had occupational therapy on Monday mornings for a while. This was tolerable and did not make our schedule seem too overwhelming because the kids' schedules were back to back (and at the same location). Dan and I got to talk to the therapists about both kids at the same time and we didn't have to run across town to different locations. Never would I dare schedule anything else on Monday mornings like doctor appointments, school meetings, etc., because I would feel like I needed to be in "two places at once" and pressured with time. This would cause me to rush out of a therapy appointment and not be involved as needed; cheating both my children and the therapists. Not feeling complete about a therapy appointment, school meeting or doctor appointment causes some inner stress and feelings of guilt. Guilt is a common feeling with autism because an autistic child takes so much time, patience and energy. When a parent feels like they haven't given adequate time, energy or patience, the guilt surfaces and adds to stress levels. So though scheduling only one appointment or one kind of therapy in one given day takes up time, energy and patience, it still allows a parent to feel like they have done all they could for that particular scheduled appointment, especially when all questions or comments are answered.

3. **Plan ahead and be organized.**
Planning ahead and being as organized as possible helps to keep the stress down. Planning for today and looking ahead to organize tomorrow makes the days run smoother, prevents rushing and hurrying around in most cases and helps save valuable time.

I always get the kids' clothes together, their book bags ready for school and plan breakfast the night before. I also make up a tentative supper menu for the week and grocery shop accordingly so I don't have to stop at the grocery store every day for one or two items.

Of course, unexpected events do happen but planning and organizing ahead lessens the anxiety of a surprise or two that may come up.

It may also be valuable to set goals of what needs to be done for the day, and for the next, to help with the organizing process. I do this a lot with housework. I clean the kitchen and bathroom daily. I vacuum every room daily. I dust the family room, bedrooms, living room and dining room every third day. I use window spray on the televisions, mirrors and inside the windows daily. This cleaning list is a given and I plan to do this list around other activities in the home. I then plan writing bills, folding and putting laundry away, etc., in between times. My husband helps me quite a bit with housework too. He knows the daily routine and helps me accomplish the goals.

4. **Know your limits.**
Knowing my limits helps to control the stress I feel as a mother and wife. If the autistic child is having a "bad" day the parents are usually in for a very demanding and stressful day. To help ease a lot of the stress, Dan and I work together as a team. If I am handling a situation with the kids and find a solution difficult to achieve, I may ask Dan to assist with or take over the situation. This gives me time to step back and catch my breath and think about how I may solve the situation if Dan continues to have problems.

If Alex, for instance, insists on eating his breakfast on the couch and not the table, I may have a difficult time getting him to understand he has to eat at the table and cannot eat on the couch. Once it seems I cannot get him to understand what I need him to do and I am feeling stressed and my patience is wearing thin, I will ask Dan to try to convince Alex of what I need Alex to do. As I watch Dan handle the situation, I will think about what I may be able to do to get Alex to understand. This will continue till either Alex eats at the table or Alex is offered breakfast later at the table.

This process of Dan and I working together helps me remain patient and not lose control therefore lessening the stress of the situation, and the day. Dan and I work together on everything. Working together means meeting half way on housework, caring for the children and handling situations that arise with teachers, therapists, etc., concerning the kids. We both contribute to decisions made for the kids as well.

Stress develops mostly from a person feeling overwhelmed and unable to "catch up." By two people working together, these feelings lessen and situations are handled with less confrontation.

5. A psychologist once told me, "Pick your battles," when it comes to handling the children. This is very valuable advice. Dan and I have set rules of the house that do not change. The kids have to put their plates in the sink when they are done eating. We enforce the rule of using "please," "thank you" and "excuse me" when appropriate. Of course the rule list goes on and on with every part of the day. By having set rules that are strictly enforced, the children know the boundaries and what they are allowed to do. Not to mention the fact that they are learning their social graces. For instance, Alex likes to empty the whole toy box. I allow him to do this as long as he helps pick up the toys and does not throw the toys around the room. Mitchell knows he can have a Popsicle when he comes home from school as long as he hangs up his coat and uses the bathroom. Danielle loves to play on my bed. She can do this as long as she doesn't touch the computer or go into my desk.

The typical rules of most households may not apply in my house, such as no snacks before supper. Mitchell is allowed to have a Popsicle when he comes home from school even though supper is only an hour away. Having a Popsicle is part of Mitchell's routine and a reward for hanging up his coat and using the restroom, both of which takes a lot of cueing on my part to get him to do. Alex is allowed to dump out the whole toy box all over the living room. I allow him to do this because of how hard it is for Alex to play with toys appropriately. My hope is he will eventually learn how to play with some toys appropriately and not break them, both on which he is improving. If he starts throwing the toys, he and I pick them up and the toy box goes into the closet.

By "picking my battles," my stress is more controlled. I don't get upset if I see Alex dump out the toy box or if I see Danielle playing with her toys in my bedroom. If I see the children doing these actions the rules are already established and it is less stressful for me to enforce the consequences. I have an appropriate, educational response already in place for rewarding and penalizing based on their actions.

6. **Accept Help from Others.**
Accepting help from others also lessens stress. Dan and I accept any help others are willing to give. In fact, sometimes the help others give seems so insignificant to them but to Dan and I it is huge. Our neighbors and my family give us the most help. When Dan and I take the kids outside, our neighbors help us watch Alex, Danielle, Adam and Mitchell, who have a tendency of wandering away. When Erik was born it was my neighbors who stayed at my house to watch the other children while Dan and I went to the hospital. It was these same neighbors who brought us dinner the day we brought Erik home. When we go to Pittsburgh to visit my family, my mom will sit with the kids and watch a movie while Dan and I eat lunch or sit down to a hot cup of coffee. When Dan takes the boys fishing, my dad will

go along and let the boys reel in the fish. At family picnics and birthday parties my sister and sister-in-law have taken Alex, Adam Mitchell or Danielle with them to feed or watch them for a while. My sister, Mary, and my sister-in-law, Angela, have scheduled birthday parties for their children together to make it easier on Dan and I who have to travel the three hours to visit them.

All of these gestures of kindness have helped Dan and I so much and have helped to relieve some stress. It is true that the simple things make a world of difference.

7. Don't Harbor Your Feelings.

There are many individuals involved with an autistic child. Sometimes this, in itself, can be very stressful. Dan and I make sure those involved with our children's care and therapy know when we are satisfied with their work and when we feel changes are needed. For instance, Alex's sensory integration therapist does a wonderful job with him. He is getting Alex to write his name and recite letters and numbers. I made sure I told Terry he was doing a great job and I told the head of the therapy department also.

On the other hand, it takes a lot of effort from Dan and I to get the kids to pick up their toys and keep all of the pieces together. Dan and I became upset when this rule was not being enforced with the TSS staff who comes into our home. Dan and I made sure we addressed our concerns and asked the TSS workers to have the kids pick up their toys and keep all of the pieces together.

This good communication of letting all involved with the kids know our true feelings helps lessen the

stress and provides trust in these important
relationships.

This is also true with Dan and I. There are times
when one, or both, of us are deeply saddened about
our children's diagnoses. At these times we make
sure we turn to each other and let all of the feelings
out into the open. Keeping feelings inside can build
stress and produces the inability to function as a good
spouse and parent.

8. **Take some personal time for yourself.**
Taking care of autistic children requires the
expenditure of a lot of energy. Sometimes this drains
us and we need time for each other and ourselves.

Hobbies help both of us find time a way from
autism and help keep our stress levels down. Dan
likes to play golf, watch and play football and read
books. I love to ride my exercise bike, play bingo and
go bowling. Together, Dan and I like to rent movies
and watch them when the kids go to bed. We try to
go to breakfast at least three times a month.
Sometimes when the kids go to bed we order take out
and enjoy eating a quite meal together. These times
together and alone are greatly needed and
appreciated. As a married couple, it is also important
to accept and support one's partner's needed hobbies.
Sometimes after an hour on my exercise bike,
stressful parts of a day don't seem to weigh as
heavily. When Dan and I enjoy a quiet take-out
dinner alone of pizza or hoagies, we usually end up
talking about the kids and what good things they did
that day. It is helpful and relaxing to simply have
someone to share time with when things seem so
overwhelming. It is also helpful sometimes to be

alone and reflect on what my life is like with four autistic children.

Stress means different things to different people. It depends upon one's life experiences. Being a parent of autistic children brings an enormous amount of responsibility. It is our responsibility to make sure the children get all they can out of school and therapy. It is our responsibility to make sure we are present for school meetings, therapy appointments, meetings with case managers and advocates and to make sure all are doing what is best for our autistic children. The busy, tight schedules we have leaves very little room for mistakes. This all causes a lot of stress, tension and overwhelming feelings on a daily basis. My husband and I run around most days not knowing when the rushing will ever stop. By the end of each week we find ourselves exhausted. But it is possible to get through a busy life schedule with the least amount of stress by simply working together, having some fun outside of autism, being honest and forthright with all those involved with the kids and by accepting help from those who love them too.

೮೦೧೩

Chapter 4
Getting in Control

There have been amazing strides made in the field of autism, and children who have it can reach great heights of improvement. The common denominator to the development of an autistic child—or any child, for that matter—has been parents who are directly involved.

In the chapter, *Dealing with Autism*, we dealt with the concept of facing autism. This sets one up to be able to now approach the subject. Confronting autism, head-on, is the best approach. And understanding it is key to being in control of it, instead of letting it control your life.

I researched and studied the subject of autism in depth. This not only allowed me to determine, for myself, that the doctors were in fact right, but it made it possible for Dan and I to get a grasp it and get in some type of control of the situation. The only alternative was to be total effect of it the situation, having no control over it; which wasn't an option if we were going to do the right thing and do all we could to help our children.

After much research, I came to know the behavioral patterns and challenges that the autistic child faces. And we started to grab the bull by the horns in getting in control of autism.

I began to make a list of traits (or problem areas) that I observed with my children with an ultimate goal of eradicating them or at least alleviating them as much as possible.

Common Autistic Traits

Autistic children usually go through the typical milestones of any child within the correct timeframe: rolling over, crawling and walking. Though there are some who are delayed with these developments, this is not as common. And a lot of times they babble baby talk just the same.

A difficult aspect of autism is that there are no precise, set-in-stone manifestations to look for. All children are different and tend to display the characteristics differently. But there are some more common traits.

Coordination: Most autistic children have difficulties with coordination. Some have gait difficulties such as with climbing up ladders or stairs. They can't understand how to move their feet and hands at the same time to go upward. They may also have difficulties with hopping, jumping, skipping and so forth. Autistic children usually have difficulties with handwriting and fine motor activities like buttoning clothing, pinching their fingers to pick up items, etc. Some autistic children never write because of their poor fine motor skills and are taught to type or only write shorter versions of things like their name and so on.

Speech: The most common pattern, and usually the first sign of autism, is the speech difficulties; both receptive (like following directions, processing what is said to them, even processing someone calling their name) and expressive. Some autistic children lose their speech around 18-24 months. Other autistic children never develop speech at all or any recognizable speech.

Mitchell was 3 years old and still babbling like a baby - not really saying anything I could understand. He never developed any speech as a young toddler.

Environmental Awareness/Alertness: Typically, what follows speech patterns is the child becomes unaware of his or her surroundings.

Inward Reposition: Another pattern is the decline of interaction with the world. Not seeking out other children for play or not wanting other children around when the autistic child plays. In some sense, the child may even ignore other children completely. My Danielle does this and young children will ask me if she can hear because it seems like she can't.

✦NOTE: The above difficulties should be based on the average capabilities in relation to the child's age. In other words, a toddler having trouble walking is to be expected. But the same difficulty at age 2 is, at least, a red flag for further investigation. Also, no one should ever jump to conclusions about their child having autism. A misdiagnosis could be very damaging to a child that didn't have autism.

Through my understanding of the typical patterns and behaviors of the autistic, I was able to recognize which problems (or challenges) Alex and Mitchell were facing, and later with Danielle and Adam. This is the first step in coming to help your child.

After distinguishing these challenges, I was able to determine what they needed to work on and what could be done to improve, or alleviate, their difficulties through the methods found in my research.

The most important thing that should be realized is there are ways of dealing with autism. And what you do in the early years can have a substantial effect on your child's entire life in how they can come to cope and co-exist in the real world. But doing nothing will increase the chances of your child's condemnation to a life of difficulty and discord, and possibly institutionalization in some cases.

I wrote down what I felt each of my children needed help with in order for them to be the best persons they could be. I divided these "issues" into categories and then developed step-by-step targets that would allow them to work their way to a final goal.

Behavior

The first area, or category, I looked at was "behavior." I asked myself what behaviors did the children have that inhibited their learning and their awareness of the world around them? Typical autistic behaviors can be biting, kicking siblings or parents, hitting others, spreading feces around a room and damaging property to name a few.

Alex would throw his food plate against the wall, put food in his hair and refuse to use silverware. He would climb the bookcase and put a VCR tape in on his own and rip them apart. I observed him spitting milk on the walls and chewing and spitting food out on the carpet.

Mitchell would follow me around the house calling my name for hours. If I told him he couldn't do or have something he would cry and scream the whole day and sometimes the next about the same issue. He would demand the same color cup or plate he had for breakfast all day. He had to have a perfect piece of cheese or cookie, no broken ones for him. I observed Mitchell always wanting to be neat and couldn't stand to spill something on his clothes or hands.

Danielle is very stubborn and wants her way all of the

time. She will tantrum for an hour if she does not get her way. The tantrums include kicking and screaming. Danielle has also been know to spread feces around her room. We have to make sure she has bottom and top pajamas on when she goes to bed.

Adam has multiple challenging behaviors. He puts everything in his mouth. He eats cardboard, wood, toys, etc. He also constantly wants to eat or drink something. Dan and I have to monitor how much he eats and drinks in a day otherwise he would be too heavy. Adam screams if he doesn't get his way, he climbs everything in the house but is very clumsy and has fallen from some pretty high places, he takes his clothes off and runs around the house naked and he has also gotten out of the house and the police had to bring him back.

Of course, the goals I set here were to stop these behaviors; the smaller step was to at least understand how to control them.

Communication

The second category was "communication." Speech is so important for anyone to be able to get along in the world. To see my children in silence was heart breaking but it was worse when I realized how frustrated they were when the words would not come out when they did begin to try to speak. For the autistic child, vocabularies are typically quite limited and need to be expanded as much as possible.

Mitchell babbled like a baby for the first three and a half years of this life. When the words and sentences started coming it was like he was born all over again. He talked sooner and better than my Alex.

Alex is still struggling at the age of five but the words are encouraged daily.

Danielle and Adam are using words and sign language to get her point across. They both will take my hand and use it to point at things they want. Sometimes both will bring me the juice and a cup to let me know that they want a cup of juice.

Encouragement is key in broadening speech inhibitions. Any word that comes out of the child's mouth, no matter how poorly articulated, should be praised and rewarded.

The two main areas I looked at with communication for my children involved *receptive* and *expressive* language.

Receptive language refers to the understanding of what is being said to the child, being able to give a germane response and to carry on a conversation and following directions.

Expressive language means words that are actually said by them; the ability to originate communication. I praise every word or sound if it is an attempt to speak. A speech therapist once told me, "If you think he said a word then he probably did say it."

My list of challenges with communication for Mitchell included:

- not saying recognizable words
- not able to follow directions
- poor articulation

Alex's list included:

- few words spoken
- not able to follow simple one-step directions
- not responding to his name

Danielle's list included:

- few words spoken
- Screaming instead of talking
- Very poor direction following – even with one

words

Adam's list included:

- Does not talk at all and screams in frustration.

- Stands in the middle of the room and will cry or scream until we figure out what he wants.

- Does not follow any directions – needs hand over hand assistance to do any tasks.

These lists were not only helpful with my own work with the children, but also came in handy when I had to give information to others who eventually came into the picture. We will cover the many areas of assistance that are available for autistic children and their families a little later.

I set my goals with each of my children with long term and short term achievements. In general, long term goals were to get these challenges completely handled while short term goals were realistic steps of minor improvement with any or all difficulties.

As a side note when setting goals, there are actually two sets, one for your child and one for you—the parent or caretaker. The goals of you and your child need to be realistic in both respects so as not to overwhelm— overwhelm your child to the point of frustration or overwhelm yourself to the point of a sense of failure on your part.

Knowing your children's strong points and weaknesses, and joys and qualms will allow you to set goals that are fair and just. And understanding your own limits and those of any assistants or therapists should be part of the equation when setting goals.

Goals can always be changed too; they are not set in stone. For someone to get it perfect the first time through is highly improbable. Stiffen or cut back on goals and steps as you see fit. After a short while, you'll be a pro at it!

Socialization

The last category involved socialization. I had never thought much about the special education preschool telling me that Mitchell was very shy and would not join in with the other children. This is because I know Dan and I are both shy people, so this seemed normal. But autism is more than shyness, and soon it became worse and more evident with my children to the point of realizing they were very different in their social skills than other typical children their age.

Mitchell was pretty aware of his surroundings but if these surroundings involved people wanting to talk to him or include him in their world, Mitchell became very anxious and would spin in circles for up to thirty minutes. Mitchell dealt with crowds by becoming loud and acting out. He did not retreat but showed a high anxiety level. I could see his pain and inability to tolerate certain situations.

Alex was very unaware of his surroundings. People could walk into and out of the room without him ever once looking up from the couch. He would not come up to anyone or acknowledge their presence. There was very little eye contact with anyone. If a room became too crowded with people, Alex would retreat to a quite place in another room. He wanted nothing to do with people at all. It was like he was in a far place and I could not reach him.

Danielle will sit in a corner and play with her doll house and little people. She will move the people in the doll house, unaware of what is going on in her surroundings. She does not want to be interrupted and will tantrum if I try to take her away from her toys to eat supper or get a bath. Danielle also likes certain movies and will watch the movie and never take her eyes off of the television despite what is going on around her. When Danielle is forced to be around people, at the swimming pool or at school, she is more like a "bully". She takes toys off of other children, pushes them away from her if they get too close and she will not share anything at any time.

Adam will immediately retreat to another room if there are visitors in our house. He will cry and pace back and forth if there are too many people around. Adam does not do well at anyone else's house and will retreat to a quiet empty room. Sometimes this is not possible when visiting others and so Dan and I do plan ahead for this. Sometimes we take him for a ride in the car or for a walk outside. Adam does not notice who is in the room, who comes and goes out of the room or what is going on around him. He loves to listen to music, especially music with a movie. He will focus on this instead of what is happening around him. He likes to steal food, drinks and toys from others and can sometimes be a bully if he wants something someone else has.

My goal for the children, of course, included helping them to become aware of their surroundings and getting them to tolerate them. The steps included, first, getting in touch with one room in the house—their bedrooms, beds, furniture and belongings, then another room—the den, their toys, the television set and furniture; the kitchen—the silverware, plates, refrigerator… to the point of all rooms and things in the house. Then their classrooms, playgrounds… their church… and so on until they were brought to observe all of their daily/weekly environments.

The positive mind set of the parents is extremely important for the child's behalf in seeing improvement. You are the stable foundation for which all achievements will build. The intention for improvement will be the driving force that moves things forward.

There is no single means to address autistic children in any aspect of their being. Finding what works best through trial and error and always doing what you as the parent feels is best for your child is the best policy. Results are always what should be the gauge and determinism should be the mindset of all who work with these children.

The Do's and Don'ts

- Always use an high-tone (happy, playful, high spirited) approach to educating your child

- Always give high praise when your child has made an achievement no matter how small it may be.

- Never "lose it" in front of your child. Remember that inability can never be wrongly identified as stubbornness. Also remember that if your child does become unruly, think of how frustrated you become when you can't accomplish something. Your child has the right to get angry at times. When this happens, take a break. Withdraw for a short while. Change the pace and go back to something that is now accomplishable.

- Always end off with a win.

- Don't expect miraculous changes. Notice the subtle ones and you will remain positive. If big changes occur, it's icing on the cake.

- Make sure there is good communication (information, progress reports, updates, changes, etc.) from all professionals who work with your children.

- Choose daycares, preschools, schools, etc., that

are eager and truly willing to work with your child.

- Praise, thank, appreciate, respect, admire, commend (and whatever else you can think of) those who are directly and indirectly involved with your child.

ॐ

Chapter 5
Assistance for Child and Family

Letting Go—Help is a Good Thing!

In the beginning, it was very difficult to allow others to work with our children. As a mother, I felt I should be doing what was best for them. But I soon realized that having others work with an autistic child in alliance with their parents was the best thing. What first caught my attention was that my children would do things for their Therapeutic Support Staff (TSS) more readily than they would for Dan or myself. And as this increased the potential for faster gains and greater improvement, Dan and I quickly became advocates of support workers being involved with the kids.

Realistically, it is impossible, if not unhealthy, for parents to be totally absorbed in autism twenty-four hours a day, seven days a week on their own. The demands of Autism can be both mentally and physically exhausting, and with the pain and heartbreak that comes with it, it is simply too much for any parent to endure alone. I learned that my emotions needed rest. It was nice to have someone else focus on and analyze my children for a while. It was good to have someone to talk to who could actually understand and have empathy for what I was experiencing. Autism is best approached by a team effort. This is the way to get the greatest results while retaining one's sanity.

After having developed a list of personal challenges and goals for my children (mentioned in the previous chapter) that I wanted to accomplish with them, I looked at strategies of how I was going to attain these goals for my kids. The socialization process was only one aspect of a larger list. Considering our limits, I knew it would be impossible to reach all of these goals with just Dan and I. This is where getting assistance is necessary and crucial in attaining realistic goals.

Case Management Support Services

Case management, by definition, is a system for delivering care which:

- coordinates

- plans

- identifies expected outcomes

- helps facilitate the patient and their family

The goal of a case management system is to:

- provide quality services
- enhance the lives of patients and their families
- make efficient use of available resources
- offer support in as many ways as possible

There are many different kinds of case management services available today. We are concerned with one that is typically called, Case Management Support Services (CMSS). CMSS is a nonprofit entity which provides community-based case management services to adults, children and adolescents with hardships such as developmental disabilities, mental retardation and homelessness.

There are divisions within CMSS that are specifically established for children who are severely challenged: Wraparound Services and Early Intervention Services.

Case Manager

The case manager is a very helpful soul. She will help in the coordination of just about every aspect of the services for the child and family. This person comes directly from Case Management Support Services.

The case manager is the child and parent's link to community resources and can be a communication system between other agencies and the parents (this includes school, wraparound agencies, special Olympics, etc). The case manager is able to discuss concerns the parent or child may have with the school (the way the child is tested, the teacher the child has, the need for more therapy in school etc) and plan meetings between the school and parents or with the appropriate individuals. The case manager and advocate can work together to make sure the family with an autistic child is provided with fair, immediate and accurate information and care for their children.

Early Intervention Services

Early Intervention (EI) provides screening, evaluation and coordination of services for eligible infants and toddlers from birth to three years of age, and their families. EI services include occupational, physical, speech and language therapies as well as psychological evaluations, specialized learning instruction and other services that may be needed for the child or family. These services can be delivered in the family's home, at a day care center or in a separate, specialized facility. (Early Intervention is similar to Wraparound Services. Much of what you read next will apply to EI as well.)

Wraparound Services

Wraparound Services start once a child receives the diagnosis of autism and can extend to the age of twenty-one years of age. They have trained individuals called Therapeutic Support Staff (TSS) who work for them in giving children one-on-one contact.

The term "wraparound" came into being around 1986 as a way of surrounding children with acute problems with "services" rather than "institutional walls." This approach is more of a process than a service as goals for improvement are set and worked toward.

The Wraparound Services TSS work on the problem areas for a certain number of hours each week, without interruptions, and develop goals of improvement to be attained. Parents are totally involved in deciding what the goals should be. This is where the "challenges" list talked about in the last chapter comes into play to the greatest extent. Wraparound agencies are funded by the state, typically, through medical assistance lines.

To get a better idea as to how Wraparound Services works, it is the PROCESS of:

- getting to know the child and his/her family

- working with them to identify their needs, figuring out, establishing and monitoring all services necessary to help improve the child's problems and, in turn, keeping the child free from any institutionalization and be free to live as normal a life as ever possible.

The actual SERVICES strive to:

- focus on the child and the family
- base the services in the home and/or community (such as with sports, boy scouts/girl scouts, etc.)
- work with all areas of the child's life (school, home life and so on)
- respect the family's culture and religious beliefs
- be the least restrictive and intrusive as possible.

The guidelines for eligibility will differ from state to state, but will likely follow similar criteria as the following:

- the child be under the age of 21

- the child be enrolled in the state's Medical Assistance Program through the Dept. of Public Welfare

- the child and family must choose to receive service (Wraparound Services cannot be mandated)

- the child must be verified by a professional (usually a doctor or psychologist) that the services are necessary to stabilize an acute situation.

The training requirements of a TSS may vary from state-to-state. In my state of Pennsylvania, they are required to have either an Associates degree with three years experience in working with special needs children or a Bachelor of Science or Master's degree in the related field of their work: special education, elementary education, occupational therapy, etc. Each state mandates their own requirements for TSS workers.

TSS personnel work on improving the child's skills and personal development as well as help to alleviate poor behavioral patterns. As a parent, there are phone calls, possibly other siblings, cleaning the house, mowing the lawn, working outside on the home, etc., which disrupt that constant time needed for the autistic child.

Wraparound Services are not offered in every state. One way of finding whether it is offered in your area is to call your local Early Intervention office. They are typically better established from state to state and would be able to direct you to any available services. If you cannot locate EI services, other places to investigate are your local health agency or education agency. Also, private agencies such as Easter Seals, have been involved in providing EI programs to children. They are associated with national and statewide associations that focus on particular disabilities or age groups. If they are not involved with autism, they may very well know who is in your area.

Another resource for finding services is through your children's hospital. Once the child has been diagnosed by a children's hospital, they can direct parents to the services that are available in the area. Many times, this is the best way of finding services in your area. The hospital will recommend a number of hours per week that Wraparound Services should spend in the home working with the child. (School hours are attained separately and will be explained shortly).

Mitchell, Alex and Danielle each have 25 hours and Adam 15 hours of home assistance with a TSS each week. The TSS workers come to our home and work with them on basic, daily living skills, socializing, speech and so forth—the things that they need work on.

Behavioral Specialists

A behavioral specialist is also a person who works for the wraparound agency or similar agency. Their credentials require having a Master's degree in the related field (special education, elementary education, psychology, etc.) that they would be working in with children.

Their job is to coordinate with the TSS workers on certain unwanted behaviors that the child has, set goals and work toward limiting or eliminating these behaviors.

An example of a goal is: my Mitchell has a difficult

time with personal skills such as dressing, bathing, toileting and so forth. Mitchell's behavioral specialist has a goal that he will have less resistance and more willingness. (Mitchell gives Dan and I a very hard time when we try to get him to do any of these types of things.)

An advocate is also very helpful at meetings and dealing with difficulties that arise.

Advocates

Since we're naming most individuals that are typically part of the team, we can't forget the advocate. An advocate is a person who is virtually an encyclopedia of knowledge on the laws of special needs kids. Some laws are statewide, while others, national. Advocates are on your side in ensuring that your child is receiving all of the benefits available as well as making sure that he/she is being treated with fairness. This can be especially helpful with special education. For example, it is a law that a school offering special ed provide transportation to children with special needs.

At one time, this was not happening with one of my children. Our advocate attended a meeting with me, bringing her personal book of regulations. She brought to light the ramifications of not supplying such transportation in compliance with the law, and the situation was resolved rather quickly. An advocate can often cut through a lot of red tape and smoke screens if they ever come up.

It can sometimes be difficult to find an advocate. The best way to find one is to ask the early intervention office coordinators, the wraparound service agency, the case management agency or simply to call your state number that supports your child's rights within the school system. In Pennsylvania there is a number anyone can call to ask questions about the laws for special needs children..

It's a Team Effort

As the intention from the parents is key, second to that is that of each individual who works to assist in the autistic child's betterment. It is the collective determinism of "the team" that will dictate the effective outcome of the child. Make sure that every person working with your child has the desire to achieve the determined goals. It is really easy for those working with your children to overlook the parent's daily challenges and only focus on the needs of the child. A professional working with your child should look deep inside the family unit, this too will be the key to true success for the child.

ဆဝ၃

Chapter 6
How to Get Assistance

The Diagnosis

The first step in receiving assistance begins with a diagnosis of autism or one of its spectrums. This is officially done at a children's hospital in the Child Development Unit (CDU).

Locate your nearest children's hospital that has a CDU and call to make an appointment. It also is good to inform your child's pediatrician or family doctor of your intentions; this doctor will be needed for assistance a lot in the future. This assistance includes prescriptions for therapies, possible letters to justify the need for equipment in the home or even a letter to verify the child's diagnosis. When speaking to the hospital's receptionist, ask for the autistic ward for diagnosing autism.

Standard guidelines have been recently developed to help identify autism in children before the age of 24 months. In the past, diagnosis of autism was typically not made until late preschool-age or even later. These new guidelines can help identify children with autism earlier, which equates to a better chance for effective treatment for the disorder.

The standardized guidelines were developed with assistance from 11 different organizations and were published in *Neurology*, a journal published by the American Academy of Neurology (AAN). According to the guidelines, all children before the age of 24 months should routinely be screened for autism and other developmental delays at their "well-child" check-ups. Children that show signs of developmental delays and other behavior-adverse signs should be further tested for autism.

The standardized guidelines developed for the diagnosis of autism involve a screening process. One of the hospital's clinicians will be looking for any of the following developmental deficiencies:

- <u>loss of</u> any language or social skills
- no babbling, pointing or gesturing by 12 months of age
- no single words spoken by 18 months of age
- no two-word spontaneous expressions by the age of 24 months (originated by the child, not simply parroting others)

A second series of testing may be given that can include medical history, neurological evaluation, genetic testing, metabolic testing, electrophysiologic testing (such as CT scan, MRI, etc.) and psychological testing as well as others.

The Recommendation

The person from the hospital who completes the diagnosis will fill out a report and, if autism or one of its spectrums is diagnosed, a recommendation for Wraparound Services will be included as part of the process.

Validate the Diagnosis

As with any important issues in life, getting a second opinion is a good thing to do. It can be found, too often, where differences in perspective can be at extreme ends of the scale when seeking professional advice. Autism, therefore, should be considered no different. Getting a second, or third, opinion is never a bad idea.

Once you feel that a proper diagnosis has been made about your child, if autism is the outcome, seeking Wraparound Services would be the appropriate next action.

Contacting Wraparound Services

The parents can simply send a copy of the hospital's report to their local Wraparound Services agency. The agency will open a file and do the necessary paperwork as a result.

Evaluation

As a result of contacting Wraparound Services, a psychologist from the agency will come to the child's home or the agency may request the child and parent to come down to their office to evaluate the child and home environment. She will talk to the child and meet with the parents in order to evaluate the current circumstances with, and surrounding, the child.

This evaluation is done solely to help determine what services the child and family may need and to verify the diagnosis of the child.. As a result of the evaluation, the psychologist will recommend a certain amount of hours of Wraparound Services (TSS assistance, behavioral specialist assistance, etc.). She will also write up a detailed report of what she has seen, first hand, and what was said to her during the evaluation. The parents do have a role in deciding how many hours they feel the child can handle also. The child's schedule will play a huge role in how many hours are feasible also (for instance, if the child naps, likes to sleep in, goes to bed early, etc).

Scheduling the Meeting

Next, a meeting is scheduled by Wraparound Services where the psychologist's findings are deliberated. This meeting is the basis for determining what services the child needs and how many hours of home and school time are necessary in assisting in the child's improvement and the family's betterment.

Therefore, when the psychologist comes for the evaluation (in the step above), it is very important that she hears about *every* issue with the child as thoroughly and detailed as possible to ensure that *nothing* is overlooked. This way an accurate picture of the situation, and the correct number of hours of assistance, can be seen by those who will adjudicate the warranting of the services for the child.

Wraparound Services Meeting

The meeting consists of a group of coordinators from the Wraparound Services agency. It is mandatory that the child's parents be present. This is because, as mentioned earlier, Wraparound Services are not mandated, they have to be condoned by the parents/guardian.

The psychologist that conducted the evaluation may not be present, and anyone who is involved with the child's care is invited—this could include: teachers, therapists, doctors, behavioral specialists, the advocate, TSS workers, case manager and anyone who the parents wish to invite that they feel will contribute to being approved for the necessary number of hours of assistance .

It is very important to bring in as many relevant individuals as possible that will weigh in favor of getting approved for assistance hours. There has been only one time that we have not been approved for assistance hours and it was the *one time* that hardly anyone from the kids' school showed up at the Wraparound Services meeting to give their input.

This meeting allows all issues to be brought up for an adequate picture to be drawn as to the complexities of the autistic child's needs. The entire group looks at all aspects of the child's life and tries to conclude what he/she needs at home, in the community and at school.

The parents have the chance to talk about their child and what goals and plans are going to be set for the TSS worker(s), who would be coming to the home and the child's school if approved for the services. There can be more than one TSS worker assigned to a child, depending on the child's needs. For instance, there could be one that is a special education teacher and another that is trained in social behavior. And as mentioned, other specialists such as a behavioral specialist, mobile therapist and so forth, can be assigned to the child as well, if it is seen to be a benefit for the child and/or family.

The psychologist talks about her findings from the evaluation to the coordinators and submits a written report.

The teachers can express their concerns over the child's needs for a Wraparound Services worker to be in the classroom with the child.

The therapists, doctors, specialists, case manager and advocate can offer any information they feel is pertinent to the child and family. Often, doctors cannot make such meetings but copies of Child Development Follow-Up Reports are sent to parents following a children's hospital annual progress development evaluation. These reports will typically give supportive recommendations of the need for Wraparound Services. A copy of this report should certainly be submitted at the meeting as well.

EVERYTHING has to be justified and properly documented. In other words, every challenge and difficulty that the child has is brought up at that meeting by the parent(s), psychologist, school representatives, anyone who has something to say. Each issue is discussed, documented and sometimes challenged. But, truthfully, everyone is there for the best interest of the child, and this is what really matters—the child's welfare.

Solutions and Remedies

From the findings of the meeting, a brainstorming stage of contriving the best ways to help with the child's needs takes place. Wraparound Services can utilize just about anything as long as it is in the child's best interest. Some services will already be in place, others will simply be things that can come from the grandparents or a sports coach, while still others will be invented if necessary. In other words, the people at the meeting join forces to find or invent services to meet every need with the following in mind:

- the needs are clearly established
- the services benefit the child and/or the family
- treatments are logical in their methodology
- services are effectively realistic

Changes to the overall plan can be made whenever necessary—and they *will* change as the child evolves.

How Many Hours is the Right Amount?

The best way of deciding how many assistance hours would be ideal for your child can be done by considering the downtime.

I feel, and many others would agree, that an autistic child can achieve the greatest improvements from the direct influence of their parents or guardians. So, first of all, figure how much time you, as a parent, can spend with your child as possible. Once you have determined your time, and stress limits, determine how much more time you feel they should be getting if someone else were to help out. *This* is the amount of hours you should request at the meeting for assistance at home.

These hours can be divided appropriately between TSS workers, a behavioral specialist, therapists, etc. In fact, to make figuring the needed number of assistance hours simpler, you can compile a list of all of your child's challenges. This can be based on your own observations as parents as well as any from the psychologist's. Then determine the level of severity of each and write down the amount of hours (monthly) you estimate for each of the challenges. Total the hours, subtract the number of hours you can spend with your child and the remainder will be the number of hours needed for assistance.

Assistance Hours for School

Obviously, if you work, you can't spend the day at school with your child. The time you feel that is needed for a TSS worker to work with your child at school must be considered and, as mentioned above, requested separately at the meeting.

Your child's teacher(s) can offer good input at the wraparound meeting on this subject. In case one or all of them can't make it to the meeting, you should always know the teachers' views on this. (The importance of being in good communication with everyone who deals with your child will be expounded on later.) Checking a week or so before a scheduled meeting is also a good idea in confirming their attendance. If one should not be able to go, request their input in writing, preferably on school letterhead, that states the teacher's views. Keep the one you receive from the teacher for your records and submit a copy of it to the committee at the meeting.

Once the assistance hours for home/community and school are estimated, you will submit them at the meeting and, like all other issues, these hours will be open for discussion. So being prepared to justify these hours can be helpful.

Recordkeeping

It is so important to keep every piece of paper you get about your child no matter how insignificant it may be and keep them altogether in a file. This file should include lots of things such as: treatment plans from Wraparound Services, therapy notes, communication notebooks from school to home, meeting notes and so on. Any and all documentation can be used as a tool to show how far your child has come and it can be a tool for justifying something (service, therapy, etc.) that your child may need. Remember each new teacher, therapist, principal, TSS worker, behavioral specialist, etc., that gets assigned to your child over time does not know how far your child has come. Sure, they may read old notes or hear information from other individuals, but they would never have all of the information that the parent would have if every piece of information received about their child were saved. Also, numerous times, Dan and I have had to prove our income hardship due to four children with autism spectrum disorders. Information kept about my children has helped me prove our financial need and hardship.

The Approval Line

The intention of Wraparound Services is to help the child and his/her family in every way possible. But the meetings are more of a fact-finding, recommendation-making caucus when it comes to receiving assistance. This is because approval does not come from this agency but a higher authority.

It is from the state level of the government that the actual approval must come. Therefore, through these meetings, a set number of hours of assistance is decided and agreed upon as being valid and appropriate for the child. As a result of the meeting, the committee submits a proposal—along with the psychologist's report and any write-ups from the parents, specialists, therapists, teachers, doctors, etc.—to the state for approval of the recommended hours.

✦NOTE: This all begins at the federal government level where special grants are delegated to state level government agencies. These state agencies are left with the authority of awarding grants, in this case—hours of Wraparound Services—to those in need of them within their relative states. ✦

The state's reply is made within four weeks of a meeting date in written form. It will include how many hours of services they feel the child should have. *So much* relies on the team's information in being sufficient and presented effectively enough to convince the state agency that the number of hours for home and school are very much needed.

Being subject to someone's adjudication that is far separated makes me nervous. I always try to have as many people attend the meetings as possible who have a lot of information and influence to give my kids the best possible chance for receiving their much needed services. As a result, as mentioned earlier, there has only been one time—knock on wood—where we have not been approved for the hours requested. And, once again, this was the one time that barely anyone from the school showed up at the wraparound meeting to give their input.

Frequency of Meetings

This meeting with Wraparound Services is held 3 times per year. The entire process is done each time from the psychologist and Wraparound Services submitting a package to the state agency for approval of hours. At each meeting, the goals that the Wraparound Services workers have been working toward for the child are discussed as well as progress, new remedies for new circumstances and other relevant issues. So the same process occurs just like the original meeting, three times each year. This means that getting approval from the state agency for the needed hours for home and school are newly granted every four months.

For my children, I go nine times a year to these meetings (Mitchell and Alex are covered in the same meeting and Danielle and Adam in another meeting) to advocate for my children to have the recommend hours of Wraparound Services that I feel are appropriate for my children.

Each time, the state will respond to a proposal submitted by the committee from the latest meeting by sending a letter of approval, or denial, before the end of the following month the meeting is held. For instance, if the meeting were to be held in January, the Wraparound Services committee would submit their proposal for hours pertaining to the months of March, April, May and June—one-third of the year. Typically, the next meeting would be held in May for services covering July, August, September and October; and so on.

✦NOTE: Approval for further services includes

showing improvement in moving toward the child's goals. So including the child's progress, not just the needs, is important. ✦

Appeals

A parent can appeal a denial letter from the state for Wraparound Services but the process takes a long time, and by the time a denial is fought, the next review period has arrived. All is not lost in a denial letter. Usually, this is not a refusal to offer assistance. It simply means they did not approve of the number of hours suggested from the meeting and will assign the hours they feel are appropriate. But if the parents choose to appeal the denial letter anyway, they must submit a letter to the state confirming their disapproval. The state will contact the parents with a formal letter when the hearing is scheduled. The wraparound agency is contacted with a formal letter also, and will usually have the hearing at their location or at the school. Everyone involved with the child attends the meeting for advocating why the hours should not be denied. A decision of how many hours granted is made at the hearing and the state confirms what was approved at the hearing by giving the parents and wraparound agency a letter in the mail.

Ironically, these hours arbitrarily recommended by the state are spelled out with so many for school and so many for home. The hours have to be used for what the state recommends them to be used for. Now does that make any sense? In my opinion, they should, at least, offer a total number of hours that could be used in the best interest of the child. This way, if more would be gained by having a TSS worker part of the time at home and part at school, this could actually be done, versus the current circumstance of having no option whatsoever for utilizing these services.

In some negotiating arenas, one might ask for more than

what they actually want. But these tactics could come back to bite you. It is best to try and request the most realistic amount of hours of Wraparound Services that would be viewed as "necessary" by the state agency. This could take a couple of meetings and responses from the state to gain some insight over you and your child, but the meeting coordinators are typically the devil's advocate on this as they are required to question and delve into the validity (or necessity) of every request brought up at the meeting. Though it can cause some frustration at times, it is the best screening process in making sure that the state's requirements are being met to their satisfaction.

Assistance is Invaluable

When a TSS worker or specialist is in our home, Dan and I can let our guards down for awhile and not have to watch that child as closely. As mentioned earlier, an autistic child needs to be kept busy and involved in the world in order to learn and improve. This is a big responsibility for parents. The wraparound assistance can help keep the child occupied, busy and improving and give you a well deserved breather.

They are not babysitters and cannot act like one. Their purpose for being there is to fulfill the goals that have been discussed and set at the wraparound meetings. For instance, Danielle is helped with managing her anger and lessening her frequency of tantrums, Alex is helped with his speech in getting him to the point of being able to ask for what he wants instead of climbing the counters in the kitchen. Mitchell is encouraged to keep on task with homework and other responsibilities. Adam is encouraged to interact with his siblings and the TSS may play a game with him and the other children in our home.

When a TSS worker goes to school with the child, they

allow for more one-on-one assistance that they often need. This can help speed progress as well as take some burden off of the teachers. While there, they cannot tell them any of the answers to their school work or help find the answers. Their job is to keep the child on task and make sure they complete their worksheets or classroom work. They can do things like help them find their classrooms and bring them through the lunch line and so forth. The TSS worker is trained on how to handle behaviors and this comes in handy in the school setting.

Autistic children have difficulties following directions and can get lost very easily with what the teacher is asking so the TSS worker can help the child follow the directions of the teacher throughout the day. All of my children have their own worker in school; even Danielle and Adam for preschool.

The schools are usually in favor of the TSS worker being present because there is less distraction for the teacher and the class. The TSS worker can make sure the child is paying attention and if the child needs to leave the room for being disruptive or to have a break, the TSS worker can take the child out of the room without interruption. Mitchell had many breaks throughout his day last year and the TSS worker knew when he needed them. Mitchell cannot tell when he has to use the restroom so the TSS worker had him on a bathroom schedule to avoid a mishap.

The psychologist, Wraparound Services, coordinators, behavioral specialist, TSS worker(s), the advocate and parents all work together to see that the child is receiving constant attention on those issues that need it.

Home Health Aids

There is a new concept brewing for special needs kids. The details are currently scarce on this service but, it involves Certified Nursing Assistants (such as those who work in hospitals and nursing homes) who come into the child's home and baby-sits the child. These individuals are called Home Health Aids. The child's medical assistance card is billed for the Home Health Aid's hours in the home. This could obviously be a great help to parents! Searching for Home Health Aids locally may reveal these services in your area. Getting approval for a home health aid for an autistic child can be tricky because having a home health aid must be deemed medically necessary.

"Is this Grand Central Station?" Dealing with it All

With Autism there is little privacy. The constant parade of professionals in and out of your home is mind boggling at times. But, it is important to remember that they are all there for one purpose—to help your child.

Once Wraparound Services are in place, a behavioral specialist and case manager may also be needed beyond the TSS worker's assistance, if they are not already part of the team. The Early Intervention or Wraparound Services coordinator should be able to fill out the necessary paperwork to get a behavioral specialist and case manager involved. Ideally, a parent of an autistic child will advocate for their child every day, with everyone. It is emotionally, spiritually and physically draining but it benefits everyone in the long run. These individuals take the parent's problems and goals to heart and will try to help with what the parent's feel are important.

TSS, a behavioral specialist, case management, possibly physical therapy, speech therapy, occupational therapy, an advocate and possibly a psychologist associated with the TSS staff, all come into the home of the autistic child and have advice or concerns they feel should be addressed (sometimes therapy is provided more in school and as outpatient therapy than in the home). This is why the goals of the parents should be clear. These professionals all are looking at the autistic child, the parents, the home schedule and structure from their professional point of view.

Some things they feel are essential may not be a big concern to the parent. The parents have to stand their ground and work with the professionals on what they feel is essential for their child. We've all heard that too many cooks can spoil the broth, and just as it is vital to have a Head Chef calling the shots in a kitchen of many, the parents are the only ones who know their child to the core—better than anyone else, and they need to hold their position when necessary.

A professional is looking at the child's outer self. A parent sees the outside and deep into the child's soul. For instance, a professional occupational therapist may feel there is a great need for the child to eat all of his vegetables before he can have a snack at night. The parent, on the other hand, may be satisfied the child is eating at all and recognize this as worthy of reward.

That the child is eating with silverware or sitting at the table for the meal may be enough as compared to earlier behavior of throwing their plate or spitting the food on the floor. The parent may see the child eating their vegetables as not a priority because there are other aspects of eating that are more important that should be praised.

Professionals working with an autistic child need to really communicate their priorities with the parent to see if maybe their goals are not really priorities at all. When a professional first starts treating an autistic child he or she needs to understand how far the child has come in *all* areas they are observing. This will allow them to make the best judgments over what is most important to work on. For instance, Alex barely spoke from 18 months until he was three years old. When he entered the special education preschool at the age of three, the speech therapist was not satisfied with Alex calling items with one word, one sound or babbling unrecognizably. She wanted sentences. I was flabbergasted when I found this out and made sure the speech therapist knew she was to never tell him he was "wrong" if he said one word or sound.

She hadn't realized how much of an improvement that babbling and making sounds were until I told her. So you can see how important it is that the parents be involved. I was excited to hear Alex say any sound. I praised him for even babbling as this was a step in the right direction. So make it clear to the professionals that work with your child where the progress is at and what your goals are—short term and long term.

The autistic child thrives on an active, regular routine; something they can count on and have some prediction with. They like everything to be predictable in their day. They need to rely on knowing what is going to happen next and feel comfortable in their "familiar" surroundings. The parents, TSS workers and other professionals all keep the autistic child as unraveled as possible, on task and involved in this world—not retreating inside of their inner world.

ॐ

Chapter 7
Education and Therapy

Education and therapy go hand in hand in improving conditions for the autistic. While therapy will typically start right after diagnosis, offering education at an early age can make an enormous difference for the autistic child. I can remember Early Intervention coming to my home for Alex, Danielle and Adam before they were even two years old. I wondered how these infants could possibly be understanding and retaining what the therapist was teaching them. But over time I began to see my children accomplish the very things that had been shown to them at that early stage. Because there is so much that must be taught—many simple activities that typical children do innately—the sooner the education starts, the better. The conventional therapies: physical, occupational, sensory integration and speech, also play an important roll in building the road for the autistic child's future. How well the education and therapy is delivered will directly influence their potential to cope and co-exist in the real world later on in life.

As an advocate of avoiding the use of drugs as a "solution" to behavioral patterns, while using patience, compassion and things that will actually increase a child's abilities, I do not favor the use of drugs on children as this is only a masking, a temporary band-aide.

Getting Them to Tune In

Before my children were old enough for school, the speech therapist, occupational therapist and special education teacher would each come to our home and utilize every possible "positive" way imaginable to get the child's attention. Whether this entailed blowing bubbles, coloring a picture or singing songs. I soon came to realize that education for the autistic child has a very broad and creative characterization.

Perception of Qualities and Characteristics

To help me better understand the way an autistic child assimilates the world, someone once explained it to me like this: A typical child sees an Oreo cookie and knows from his or her own observation that it is the same as a chocolate chip cookie—both are cookies, they can be eaten and taste yummy. The autistic child does not know what an Oreo or a chocolate chip cookie is or that both can be eaten or they taste yummy until someone renders the child to come to know this.

Everything is taken literally, so the world is seen as being very structured and in a narrow context. There are many types of dogs, cats, doors, windows, houses, bathrooms, ad infinitum. The autistic child needs to be exposed to as much of the world as possible *in all its variety* in order to come to know as many of these differences as possible. This formidable task will make life more tolerable through better adaptation to their surroundings.

A typical child is born with the notion that a fish comes in many shapes, sizes, colors and so forth, but whatever the differences, they are still understood to be fish. An autistic child may see a goldfish and with their literal mind understand a fish to always look like *that* particular goldfish. The autistic child needs to be brought to understand that a fish is a broad category of many like forms. In other words— **differentiation (the ability to tell the difference between things) is, to a greater or lesser degree, missing from an autistic child's self-determined comprehension.**

It is up to the parents, therapists, teachers, coaches… to *show* these differences to the autistic child. Almost anyone can help immensely—siblings, family, friends, whoever comes in contact—simply by knowing this one key factor and therefore introducing the different hues of the world to the unsuspecting child.

The education does not only entail numbers, letters, colors and shapes, it is understanding what the autistic child faces in the environment daily. The professionals who came to the house when my children were not yet two years old helped shape their lives in many different ways. I know these individuals had an impact on my children; I see it in their eyes, I see it in their awareness. I can still picture them mimicking the professionals' approaches and words.

There were never any miraculous changes but slight differences, which I live for daily. Many of the results of the professionals' efforts, like I've mentioned before, are not always seen in a day, a week, a month or even a year. But they show up over time with patience, love and determination.

Communication: Knowing What's Going on with Your Child is Key

One thing I demanded when my children were receiving

Early Intervention services and once they attended the special education preschool was information. There must be ample communication between all professionals who see the children and their parents. By "all" I mean all therapists, TSS workers, behavioral specialists, case managers, teachers, advocates and so forth. If the person is involved in your child's care there must be communication with you – the parent. This also includes daycare professionals and babysitters. This communication can be by way of written narratives, check lists, face-to-face meetings or phone calls.

I have communication notebooks for all my children and I try to speak with the teachers and aids at least once a week. Keeping in touch is vital because this is the only way a parent knows:

- how the child is progressing,
- what behaviors need work
- what academics seem to be a problem.

Sometimes, I would find professionals who didn't understand my strong desire to know what was going on with my children in school. It is up to the parent to ask, and politely insist on it if necessary. This could be accomplished in as simple a manner as asking questions to what you want to know about your child. You could start out with general questions such as:

"How did she do this week?" or "How did he behave?" to more specific questions like,

"Did she accomplish what we were going for?" or "Did he talk today"" "What did he say?" and so on.

A lot of times the professionals get engrossed into their busy schedules and forget **how vital the parent's role in education and therapy is**. When Mitchell was four, he would sometimes come home from the special education preschool very agitated. He would wander around the house nonstop. Dan and I could not figure out what was going on with him. He wanted nothing in particular. I would offer him food, drinks, a story, etc., but he would continue to be restless. After speaking with the special education preschool people, I found out they were using a weighted blanket with Mitchell in school. They'd found when he was restless and agitated that he was needing some sensory pressure (which will be covered later).

They would put him under the blanket for some "down time." Dan and I tried putting him under a heavy sleeping bag and this did help him. After this he was calm and happy. We also received some information from the occupational therapist about what to do with deep pressure to calm him when he would become restless or agitated. So by getting into communication with the preschool, we were able to learn of a successful way to help our child feel more comfortable.

At that time Mitchell had only been diagnosed with autism for 10 months. Dan and I were still learning and knew nothing about deep pressure for calming. And we would still be in the dark if we hadn't asked questions. The moral here is: **don't expect anyone to volunteer their information. Be assertive and stay in tune to what is being done with your child.** If the school would have shared their knowledge with us, Mitchell would not have had to go through this unnecessary discomfort at home.

And just the same, the teacher might not know about some situation and could, unwittingly, upset the child. Informing the teacher about it could keep your child from unnecessary anguish.

Insist on knowing what is going on even when things are going really well. Shedding a different light on this, knowing what to do allows you to be in control of situations. Not knowing what to do to help your distressed child is very painful and stressful on the parents.

Also, just as with any child, leaving teachers to raise our kids is never the answer. It takes a collaborative effort which requires major input from the parents. The same goes for autistic children—even more so. The more input of assistance (teaching, comforting, etc.) the child receives, the greater chance they have for advancement.

Your Goals

Your goals for your child are important too and need to be taken into consideration. I used to have the Early Intervention staff mail me notes on Danielle. This was very nice. Once a week I received written notes and a phone call about her progress. Communication can be exhausting at times and very time consuming but it is priceless information for verifying just how the child is truly doing. Knowing how things are going allows you to base appropriate decisions for your child's best interest. Education is vital in all ways and ensures some hope for the future.

IEP Meetings

As with Wraparound Services meetings, parents are involved in the Individualized Education Program (IEP) meetings as well. These meetings are held annually upon initial assessment or when the student has a lack in anticipated progress, upon request by a parent or teacher or when something with the child's program needs to be revised or rewritten. These meetings are structured around goals being set for an autistic child in school.

Listen and Make Requests

At these meetings, listen carefully and ask a lot of questions.

✦NOTE: A note to professionals: It is important to

remember that parents need time and explanation of every step of the process, even if they have been at an IEP meeting before. ✛

As a parent, you have the right to ask for written goals or summaries from the different disciplines attending the IEP meeting before the meeting date. I have found IEP meetings to be helpful but also hurtful: helpful because they give me a sense of where my children are headed or how well they were doing in class, hurtful because I am told negative things such as what they are not doing or achieving.

There should be no major surprises at the IEP meetings if there is already good communication established. My advice to parents who plan to attend a meeting is the following:

- Take someone with you who is another professional (especially an advocate or a behavioral specialist, case manager, TSS, therapist) that knows and agrees with your goals for your child.

- Have a list of your goals to be addressed. One of your goals should be the desire to have some kind of communication between you and the school.

- Stand your ground on what YOU want for your child.

- Make sure the professionals who work with your child that you want to attend the meeting are present. If they do not show up parents can request an additional IEP meeting or a continuation of one until all professionals have had a chance to discuss their goals and hear the parents' input.

- Taking notes of the IEP meeting is helpful for a parent to remember what was said. It is also very helpful for the teachers and therapists working with the child in school. They have a lot of children to work with and there is the possibility of a mix-up or things that should be being done are left out. If it has been stated in the meeting but not on the IEP minutes, your notes are the only way you can verify that what has been discussed is certain to be written up in the IEP report and a part of your child's program.

Once the meeting is over, the parent should give a photocopy of the IEP minutes to the attending advocates and go over all the notes. All important issues about the child should be covered even if the issues do not happen a lot at school. For instance, my Alex has gotten out of our house before. He crawls out windows and unlocks even the best dead bolts on our doors. This is a common trait for an autistic person. One time he was lost for an hour. We had to call the police. They found him 2 blocks away. Alex is not safety aware or very verbal. He darts across streets, cannot tell anyone where he lives and would go with anyone. I was terrified.

We did finally find him that day. Now our house has a security system and we have locks on top of the doors (see chapter on safety for more information on how to safeguard autistic children). I made absolutely sure the school knew that Alex is impulsive and capable of running off. Because of this, he has a TSS and very on-guard aids in the classroom who keep an eye on him throughout the day.

If an issue is forgotten or not talked about at the meeting, the parent should make sure the school or professional is somehow made aware of the overlooked issue.

A meeting with each of the therapists individually is also helpful after an IEP meeting to ensure all information is accurate and the goals are realistic and appropriate. This does not have to be a formal meeting. You can call the school and ask to come in and speak with the speech therapist, occupational therapist and so on. The notes taken at the IEP meeting can be discussed and appropriate goals worked out.

This individual meeting is very helpful because on the IEP meeting day the attendees get a few moments to speak about their problems, goals and interventions being reviewed. The parents and professionals need to be on the same page at all times for the child to get the maximum benefit otherwise, each could be undoing the other's work and progress could be slowed. But this meeting reveals any counter-efforts.

The Parent-School Liaison

The autistic child's advocate and case manager should be used for communication between the parent and the school. These individuals should make frequent visits to the child's school to help teachers and the principal with any concerns or questions. The advocate and case manager can then relay any messages or issues to the parents. This helps make the communication line more effective. Taking them to the IEP meeting is helpful because they have a great deal of experience with these meetings and can offer good advice and help with how to proceed.

Schools typically invite any help with making the autistic child's school year more successful. Also, a parent can become exhausted and numb when dealing with so many daily difficulties inherent with an autistic child. Having someone else there eases some of the worry that something important will be forgotten.

I rely on my advocate and case managers to tell me how my children are honestly doing in school. I depend on them to deal with any problems that may arise and help me communicate my concerns on behalf of the children.

For instance, Mitchell was having so many difficulties the first four weeks of kindergarten. He was anxious and very restless. He was rocking back and forth in his chair, banging his head with his fists, talking uncontrollably and he would not comply with doing his worksheets. All of these behaviors were unlike him and very new. I turned to the behavioral specialist who tried timeout and other disciplinary tactics but the behaviors continued. She felt it was more of a sensory issue (sensory will be talked about shortly). And after taking Mitchell to see a psychologist, I realized he was very stressed and nervous. He was in a new school with a new teacher. Too many changes all at once for him. I contacted an occupational therapist who specialized in sensory integration. This therapist put Mitchell on a special program to ease him into his day. This did wonders for Mitchell; he was a whole different kid in school after that.

The cooperation between the advocate, case manager, behavioral specialist, the school and myself made this possible—all founded by good communication. The school staff should be thankful for someone coming with the parents to the IEP meetings because it does open up the lines of communication and things do go more smoothly. If there is objection to this, you need to find out why because there should be no opposition in the betterment of your child.

Before going to an IEP meeting for one of my kids, I always go out to breakfast with my husband and discuss the various goals we feel are vital for our child. I brought these goals to the meeting and stood my ground for why these objectives were so important to us. School staff present at the IEP meeting have always been thankful for our input because it is clearly understood that the parents know the children best. If the goals were left solely up to the professionals without the parents' input, the goals would remain at a high or general level and the personal goals (relating to the child) would be left out.

Every autistic child has difficulties with expressive (speaking to others) and receptive (listening to others) speech, socializing and gross and fine motor activities to name a few. These difficulties warrant goals but these situations have underlying problems that require specific, more refined goals. For instance, Danielle has exceptionally poor receptive speech. She cannot follow a simple, one-step command. On the personal side, she has difficulties following directions because she is so absorbed inward into the autistic world. Danielle is the hardest to reach out of my four autistic children. She does not follow directions well or speak very well because she does not want to be so much involved with the outer world—her environment. When I went to her IEP meeting I discussed this heartrending characteristic to the board of professionals' present. It was at this time I made a decision that she would receive group activities less often than she would with one-on-one activities. One-on-one works better because the other person can keep her on the task at hand and guide her all the way through it, inch-by-inch. In group activities, Danielle can zone-out and sink into the autistic world more readily. The point being, if I had not added my personal twist to the goal, Danielle's goal would not have been as personal for her specific needs in this area. The goal would simply have been made to get Danielle to follow directions. This would have been too general and could have possibly created drawbacks or no results. But now she has someone focusing on the more specific issue and pushing her through the program no matter what and keeping her focused. Danielle is only in preschool at this time but, maybe, by the time she goes to kindergarten in two years, she will be more in tune with the world around her.

I have been to IEP meetings before where some of the professionals that were needed in the discussion were not present. This makes developing goals very difficult. Parents can ask whether everyone is going to be present. Like stated earlier, parents can request more than one IEP meeting and continuations of one until all professionals have had a chance to discuss their goals and hear the parents' input. IEP meetings should be set when the parents and other professionals are able to come. The IEP meetings are usually set up by the school whenever the annual anniversary comes around. A meeting can also be requested by the parent at anytime during a school year. It is best if this request is put in letter form and mailed to the school principle or special education coordinator. This person, in turn, should call the parents and schedule an IEP meeting when all can be present. Usually the school contacts the parents only. It is up to the parents to contact the case managers, behavioral specialists, TSS, advocate, etc., for making sure they make it to the meeting as well.

Conventional Education with Special Ed

Education for an autistic child does not have to be only "special" education and therapy. It can be a typical setting with a TSS or aid. I never knew this until my Mitchell was in kindergarten. No one had bothered to tell me. All that time I kept Mitchell in special education only. Once he went to regular kindergarten with his typical peers he blossomed. By mid year he was reading at a second grade level. He could name all his letters with sounds and count to one hundred. Imagine what he could be doing if I would have put him in regular preschool and special education earlier.

Choosing the Right Classroom Setting

An autistic child has difficulties with different settings so a regular preschool or school classroom setting must be chosen carefully. I put Alex into a regular preschool at a nearby catholic school when he was four years old. The preschool was too structured and stimulating for him. He would walk out the door frequently while he was there because it was too much. Dan and I had to teach the teacher about autism day-after-day. It was very depressing, disappointing and exhausting for us and very stressful for Alex too.

We removed him after one month. The teacher and principal were concerned about our decision but Dan and I were confident we had done the right thing. We then enrolled Alex into a preschool program at a nearby daycare center. The fruits of our decision became apparent when we saw Alex learn to say his shapes and colors and began to count. He really improved there because they were willing to make him fit in. There were only eight kids in the class and the teacher spent a lot of time with Alex. This setting worked out better because this is what he personally needed.

Danielle, when she was three years old, attended a regular, age three preschool and the special education preschool as well as outpatient therapy at the local hospital once a week. The regular preschool was difficult for her but she had an aid who spent one-on-one time with her throughout the day. Her teacher and the other three-year-olds treated her wonderfully. Danielle hates being forced to do something and would yell and throw tantrums but the teacher and other students simply helped her along. Unfortunately, Danielle did not progress in her academics nor did her behaviors improve by the end of the preschool year. The following year Dan and I chose to put her in all special education classes where her behaviors could be better managed and the professionals were more able to develop strategies to overcome the behaviors, which were a huge barrier to her learning. By the end of this school year Danielle was like a different child. In this case, the special education preschool, for Danielle at four years old, was the best choice for her.

In the special education preschool the child is exposed to the same classroom and teacher for two to three years (this may differ in other areas). Sometimes the regular school setting, in addition to special ed., can help an autistic child simply by their learning to tolerate being around others in new environments. The children need different environments and to be around typical peers their age. My four autistic children were into four different schools at one time.

This was very confusing and overwhelming at times. My kids' advocate and case managers helped us out so much by visiting them in school settings and helping us keep up with what was going on.

Some autistic children cannot function in a regular school setting but as a parent, look at every option. Sometimes head start or daycare preschool settings are willing to work with autistic children. Remember education is not only academics. It is learning about the environment and everything simple in the world as well.

Dealing with Change

Though combining schools may often be good for autistic children, change is very difficult for them. The most traumatic is changing schools, whether it be from preschool to elementary or elementary to middle school to high school. One driving force for success for the autistic child, as is with any child, is routine—sameness and comfort. A new school introduces a strange, unpredictable environment, which generates discomfort and insecurities.

Some ways to ease the uncomfortable feelings is to take your child to the new school far before the new school year begins, meet the principal and allow the child to walk around with you through the hallways and into the classroom(s) that he/she will occupy when enrolled. If possible, let the child play with a couple of toys or experience some type of enjoyment in the classroom. Keep in contact with the school before your child begins there. All of these things will help to familiarize your child with the new space and any pleasurable experience that can accompany this will only make the transition that much easier.

The child should be exposed to the new school as much as possible before the new school year begins. I had Mitchell sit in on a kindergarten class the April before he started. He met all the kindergarten teachers and saw their classrooms. He visited the new school once a week from May until August. He visited the principal's office, the library, the gym and the cafeteria. We would drive by the school and say with enthusiasm, "There is Mitchell's new school and kindergarten!" This helped Mitchell feel more comfortable. When school started, there were still difficulties but the school year went much smoother because we had prepared him. The principal, special education coordinator and office secretaries all knew me by name. I made sure the communication lines were wide open early on. I also made some suggestions to the principal for Mitchell that he welcomed. This principal will be with Mitchell for the next six years and the relationship I forged with him will make these years much easier for everyone.

At the special education preschool I know everyone right up to the top including the special ed coordinators, board members and area supervisors. When I call with a question, suggestion, compliment or complaint, everyone knows who I am and who my kids are. Yes—I included "complaint." In striving for positive change, it is possible to get caught up in the endeavor, always working for improvement no matter what. The "no matter what" part can sometimes come off as rude or a putdown to others, though it is not meant in that way, or simply a struggle between two individual's views. One can say, "Such is life in all walks," and this would be true. But the efforts made by those who are working with your child cannot go without recognition, if only for the fact that their activity with your child could have the potential of being reduced to a chore instead of a goal. Not to mention that it is the right thing to do for someone who is working hard for you. Notice that "compliment" is also included in the types of calls I make. **It is important to acknowledge the good things that everyone does for your child.** Praise, thank, appreciate, respect, admire, commend (and whatever else you can think of) those who are directly and indirectly involved with your child. Noticing the good deeds of others is magical in its ability to fortify advocacy, not to mention it makes life more enjoyable.

Before an autistic child begins in a new school it is good to keep the school informed. I always had a contact person at the schools my children were going to be attending that I could talk to. If anything came up that I wanted to discuss I talked with them. When Danielle started into special education preschool I spoke to her teacher about everything. I kept her informed of every outpatient therapy session, the results or lack of, and every behavioral problem at home. The information was well received and helped keep things consistent between home and school.

What to Look For in a Daycare Center

Leaving an autistic child in the hands of a daycare center requires a personal inspection into the capabilities and expertise of the facility. Each autistic child is different and the approach to daycare should be a very thought-out endeavor. A daycare setting can be too stimulating for an autistic child, and due to the child's poor social skills and auditory processing, the child could be put in too stressful of an environment. The safety measures a parent has in place in the home may not be possible in a daycare setting. The autistic child may not be able to have the one-on-one attention needed in the daycare setting. Parents may find themselves educating daycare personnel about autism, sensory difficulties and poor safety skills continuously.

On the other hand, an autistic child who is more high-functioning may find a daycare setting a good educational experience. The child may enjoy learning the social and playing skills of their typical peers.

This child may enjoy the structure and set routine of an institutional environment versus a daycare setting.

For me, a daycare center was out of the question. My children will not sleep or eat anywhere else but home, unless Dan or I are present. Also, the safety awareness of my children is very poor. They need constant supervision and the responsibility is just too much to ask of others. Even Mitchell, who is more high-functioning, needs help with safety awareness, socially appropriate behavior and self-help skills like dressing, toileting, bathing, etc. Mitchell needs a bathroom schedule as he does not know when he has to go to the bathroom.

Improving Skills with Therapy

Incorporating education with therapy is invaluable for increasing the autistic child's chances of having as normal a life as possible in the real world. If we were to delineate their differences for our purposes here, "education" could be described as teaching for **understanding** while "therapy" is training someone to **do**. Education gives information to impart knowledge about things; therapy coaches in order to accustom someone to a form of behavior or performance.

Speech Therapy

Speech therapy is an essential part of an autistic child's improvement. It is based on direction following and helps build the auditory processing which can improve over time. Sometimes it also improves as the child matures and becomes more involved with the world. I have seen improvement in auditory processing with my Mitchell, Alex, Adam and Danielle, a lot in the last 3 years. This has made me very proud!

The child not only requires assistance with expressive speech but also needs help naming and pointing to pictures, following directions (auditory processing) and finding a way that fits that particular child to communicate whether it be the picture exchange system, sign language, real objects and some other method that works best.

The Picture Exchange System

The picture exchange system is a very popular form used to initiate communication and verbal speech. This method uses pictures to develop one-word requests and eventually sentences to help build verbal skills. I have found it very useful for my Mitchell. He loves seeing the pictures fit together into a sentence and started verbalizing sentences very quickly with it. It also helped him learn how to communicate what he wanted. Prior to the picture exchange system, Mitchell would stand in the middle of the kitchen and whine. He knew what he wanted but made no verbal attempts or gestures to clue Dan or I to what it was. We could not understand him.

The picture exchange system worked for Mitchell because he could visualize the sentence in his head and eventually ask for what he wanted. This system was not, however, successful at home for Alex, Danielle or Adam. But in a school setting it did work very well. Alex and Danielle are two very independent kids anyway. They know how to go to the refrigerator and get a drink, to grab a cookie from the cupboard and get their coats and shoes to go outside. Adam is just starting the picture exchange system and his main difficulty is focusing on what he needs to do.

In the home setting Danielle and Alex were used to getting Dan's and my attention by bringing us what they wanted or getting it all on their own. Adam will take my hand and direct me to what he wants in the home. Mitchell lacks the inspiration to be independent; he always has, so the picture exchange was very useful for him as he enjoyed talking and asking for what he wanted.

Other ways of communication involve many different electronic devices that can be adapted to the home environment as well as the use of sign language. Sign language did help my Alex, Adam and Danielle because they connected the hand movements with the words. He used this with verbal words and this helped to develop his verbal skills too.

Auditory Processing

Auditory processing difficulty is a very common characteristic of autistic children. Auditory processing means a child hears what is said to them, it is processed in the brain or mind and an immediate response is seen with a reaction of some kind. Such as when a parent says a child's name, the child hears it, the brain processes it and the child turns his/her head in the direction of the calling parent as a response. In the autistic child, the auditory processing is delayed. It can be severely delayed or may only take a few seconds to process the information and respond.

If Mitchell is asked what he did in school, some days he does not answer. Other days after about twenty seconds he may give a response. It is in his IEP write-up at school that the teacher will give Mitchell adequate time to process the information and give a response. The teacher is not to hurry him along or expect a response instantly. Doing so causes unnecessary pressure and can deter communication altogether. A child not responding to their own name is the first red flag of auditory processing difficulties and "possibly" the incidence of autism. This was our first signal something was not right with Danielle. Even though it was hard to imagine something being wrong with her too, when she stopped responding to her name, I already knew what it was in my heart.

Physical Therapy

Physical therapy helps with autistic children on balance, coordination and body awareness issues. Mitchell, Danielle and Adam see the physical therapist in school a half hour per week. This has helped them immensely. They all now alternate their feet going up and down stairs instead of always leading with the same foot. They can catch a ball with their hands, jump, hop on one foot and step over items in the center of a room. These types of activities might seem trivial until one sees the child struggle with simple things like climbing a ladder (having difficulties moving their hands and legs at the same time), stepping over objects and swimming.

Occupational Therapy

Occupational therapy works on handwriting (holding a pencil correctly), dressing with buttons and zippers, tying shoes, manipulating small objects like beads onto a string and stacking blocks in various ways to avoid ritualistic play. Ritualistic play is when a child plays with something the same way every time. For example, a child may be given colored rings to put on a post. The autistic child may put the red on every time first, followed by the yellow, then the blue, then the orange. In ritualistic play, every time the child puts those colors on a ring, they would be placed on in the same order. Occupational therapy can help a lot with activities of daily living like bathing independently, potty training, dressing, combing ones hair and brushing teeth. These activities are not normally done in a school setting but can, and should, be done at home if these activities need fine tuning. Mitchell received home occupational therapy the whole summer before kindergarten to help with the activities of daily living and to motivate him to be more independent. The therapist helped Mitchell with sequencing activities like dressing, using the bathroom, brushing his teeth and so forth. This did seem to help him. Every autistic child is different, like I have said many times already, and teaching the child to be independent with dressing, bathing, toileting, brushing teeth, etc., comes with much repetition and a very routine-like schedule. Mitchell, for instance, is able to put his clothes on, use the bathroom, brush his teeth and bathe himself, but he needs cues with each and every step. Alex can also dress himself, bathe himself and brush his own teeth when the clothes are put out for him, the toothbrush and toothpaste are set up and a wash cloth has soap already on it. Alex needs little encouragement because he is so motivated. Mitchell needs much encouragement because he has little desire to be independent. Danielle and Adam are still totally dependent for all of their daily living skills. With the same schedule followed everyday with the same routine, Danielle and Adam will learn to participate more with my encouragement as time goes on. The autistic child's ability to follow directions correlates with their ability to do more for themselves also. And, though mentioned elsewhere in this book, it is so important to say again: every time an autistic child does what a parent, caregiver, therapist, teacher, etc., wants him/her to do, the child should be praised. This also creates good results.

Of course these are just a few examples of the many things that occupational therapists, speech therapists, sensory integration therapists, physical therapists and specialists do. They use numerous strategies and have many goals for the child. The goals are individualized to suit each child's specific needs.

I cannot begin to say how important each of these therapists are to the autistic child's future. Both parents, if possible, should be closely involved with the therapists. They should be in communication all of the time about the child's progress. As mentioned before, they need to make sure these individuals know the goals that have been set and are willing to work toward attaining those goals. If the therapist and child do not have a good relationship, it is vital that you find another therapist. An autistic child can have difficulties with a certain therapist for reasons that may be unclear to the parents and the therapist. It is VERY important that all involved are in sync when it comes to therapy. Otherwise, things could go too slowly or even slip backwards.

Communication is so important for all involved with the child. Education through academics and therapy is the only way an autistic child has real hope for the future. The parents have an enormous responsibility—the responsibility to make sure their autistic child is getting the best education and therapy possible.

ॐ)ॐ

Chapter 8
Sensory Integration

I have heard my children described as many different adjectives: lazy, manipulative, stubborn, impulsive, impatient.... These terms have been used by individuals who do not live, nor experience autism on a daily basis. Autism is very complex. A parent almost has to be a scientist who researches why an autistic child behaves in a certain manner day after day. Sensory integration plays a key role into why autistic children behave the way they do and how they perceive the world.

Sensory Integration Dysfunction was first identified by an occupation therapist named Anna Jean Ayres in the 1960s. In 1972, Sensory Integration International, a nonprofit organization, was established to further Ayres' work with sensory integration therapy.

Sensory integration is the ability to take in information from the environment through the senses – touch, smell, taste, vision, hearing and also movement – and put it together in the brain and make a meaningful response.

Sensory dysfunction occurs when the brain is unable to process the information from the environment properly, therefore inappropriate responses result. Some characteristics of sensory integration dysfunction are: attention and regulatory problems, sensory defensiveness or under reactive to sensory stimuli, unusually high or low activity patterns and poor organization of behavior. (These are explained below).

The ability to concentrate on a task is disrupted with sensory dysfunction. Attention and regulatory problems interfere with learning and independence. In order to attend to task an individual must have the ability to screen out nonessential sensory information and background noises. With sensory dysfunction, a child has difficulties with the screening process and reacts. This reaction makes the child seem hyper and distractible. The child has difficulties attending to therapy sessions, classroom activities and daily living skills. Alex has such a hard time with attention span. We have difficulties getting him to sit at the supper table, dress himself and even to use the toilet. Although he has a poor attention span he can still attend to certain activities, but not to others. For example, he will sit and build a birdhouse out of wood but will not sit at the supper table for more than three minutes. He will sit and watch a two-hour video but will not sit in his car seat for a half-hour ride. Sometimes this behavior makes the child look "manipulative." A teacher told me one time, "I think he can sit at circle time. He just doesn't want to." This could be true but chances are his difficulties in keeping on task are interfering with his abilities to do what his teacher wants him to do. Once Alex receives some sensory integration therapy he has a better chance of sitting and doing what someone may ask of him.

As an important side note: it is important to differentiate between an autistic child and one that has had a lot of sugar through candy, cookies and other sweets or even from juice drinks with added corn syrup/fructose/etc. and things like soda, which have sugars and even caffeine. If you don't believe this possible, observe a group of children, or just your own child prior to having no sugar-related food or drink. Then introduce sugar and see the difference in their behavior. The change will amaze you. You will see them turn into loud, obsessively running around, and sometimes even ornery and disobedient kids within just a few minutes. The inability to sit still for lengthy periods for a child can be a challenge simply because they are kids – even without the influences of sugar – and their hunger for new and different things is almost insatiable. None of these things should be mistaken for autism, nor a hundred other "abnormalities" or "disorders" labeling our children today so readily. I would recommend as a very first response to indications of autism or if someone labels your child with some "hyper active" disorder, ensure they are not being misread by stopping the child's intake of sugars and caffeine.

Regulatory Difficulties Regulatory difficulties entail difficulty with eating and sleeping, and an inability to calm or console oneself. Many autistic children have trouble sleeping. This may include not sleeping well or the child needing an excessive amount of sleep to function. My autistic children all slept ten to twelve hours at night. When they were younger and napped, they took a three-hour nap and slept at least ten hours a night. I can remember Dan and I working everything around naptime including family visits, doctor appointments, etc. If they missed their nap or did not sleep at night for whatever reason, Dan and I had a very stressful day.

All my autistic children have different eating habits. Mitchell will eat nothing that looks "messy" like spaghetti, soup, lasagna, etc. Danielle and Adam eat something one night for supper but may not eat it again for a few months.

Alex eats hot dogs for breakfast and French toast for supper.

I have only "healthy" foods in my home mainly because I do not make food an issue. Due to various difficulties, sensory issues being one, the kids do not necessarily eat three meals daily but six to eight small snacks. Getting them to sit and eat is difficult so if they sit and eat snacks throughout the day, then at least they are eating.

Another regulatory difficulty for some autistic children is the ability to console oneself after something makes the child sad or angry. Danielle is hard to sooth or console when she is upset. She will tantrum and cry for hours about one small thing. She will have a tantrum about anything and everything, especially if she disagrees with the authority figure's answer to what she wants. She has difficulties letting go of the emotion and moving on. She stays focused on that emotion and will think about it for hours to even days later. She can be still moody and throw a tantrum when something reminds her of that particular emotion. This makes it difficult to pin point what she is so upset about and how to handle the situation. This can be very frustrating for the parent and the child. Many methods are used to console her. Sometimes she will not allow me to hold or comfort her. Other times she seeks me out for this. It depends upon her need at the time.

This is something that takes time to learn and teach others. Dan and I get many stares because of Danielle's screaming and crying. Each child is different, but if a tantrum can be predicted, the professional or child should still continue with the rules and not give in to the inconsolable child. The rules have to be enforced and eventually the tantrums will lessen and dissipate. On the other hand, a parent or professional must weigh the need to enforce or give in to what the child may want. For example, Danielle may tantrum in school whenever playtime is over, especially because she has to put away her favorite baby doll. What is wrong with bringing her favorite baby doll to the table with her and then when she is shown the snack asked to give the baby doll up for her snack? The answer is, "Nothing is wrong with this." It just makes common sense to deal with any child this way: take their attention off of the item with a new item you want the child interested in. Taking something away abruptly simply isn't a fair thing to do to a child. Just think for a minute how you would feel, even as an adult, if someone took your purse or wallet without your consent. Not a good feeling, is it?

One of Danielle's challenges is following directions. This is especially difficult whenever she must move from one thing to another. Because of the difficulties of following directions, a verbal reassurance of what comes next is not enough. She must see and hear what is next. Letting her see the snack and then decide to give up the baby doll prevents tantrums and a breakdown of confidence in the person making the change. Danielle gives up the baby doll easier and easier each time this technique is used with her.

Sensory Defensiveness

Sensory defensiveness is a sensory dysfunction where the autistic child cannot tolerate being touched or exhibits a reaction to something in the environment that most would consider harmless. "Tactile defensiveness" is defined as hyper responsiveness to touch. The nervous system is highly aroused and a simple touch can be defined as painful for the autistic child. A child who exhibits sensory defensiveness can show behaviors like aggressiveness, avoidance, withdrawal and intolerance to daily living routines. This is the child that cannot tolerate a parent brushing or shampooing their hair, their face being washed or someone brushing their teeth. The parent can become frustrated with the constant tantrums when the daily living skills are being done. Danielle cannot stand touching shaving cream or finger paints. And when I take her to get her haircut, I make sure no one else is in the store because Danielle screams and cries the whole time. Mitchell cannot stand anything touching his lips when he eats. He bites food such that nothing touches his lips. If the food touches his lips he will not eat that food again. Alex cannot stand his clothes being wet. If he goes sled riding or has an accident in his pants he cannot tolerate the wet clothes on his skin. Adam loves hugs but only when he initiates the hug. He does not like to be touched unless it is on his terms.

Auditory Defensiveness

Auditory defensiveness is the sensitivity to sounds and certain noises. Some children are sensitive to the toilet flushing or a ceiling fan. Some lights in school have a small buzzing sound that may be unnoticeable to most students but to the autistic child this can be very distracting. Mitchell cannot tolerate the sound of thunder, carnival rides, the fire drill at school, live concert bands, airplanes and many people talking at once. Alex does not like the sound of a smoke detector and fire trucks. Adam does not like the sound of the hair dryer or the vacuum running. Danielle does not like the sound of many people in a room together. She, just like Mitchell, cannot concentrate in school when all the children say the Pledge of Allegiance of the flag together or reciting the months of the year and the days of the week together

This is very common in autistic children, the sound of many people talking at once is loud and garbled. If a sound is bothersome an autistic child can have a huge tantrum or hyper reaction. All teachers, therapists and parents should be aware of what sounds bother a child and how to either prepare the child for the sound or take the child away from it. In kindergarten, Mitchell is taken outside of the school before the fire drill goes off. He cannot tolerate the sound. When a storm is coming or it starts storming I sit with him and we watch cartoons together.

Visual Defensiveness

Visual defensiveness occurs when an autistic child is sensitive to light. This happens a lot in school. The florescent lights are very tiring and can be a distraction to the autistic child. Mitchell has the lights above his head in school turned off. If at all possible the child should be placed in a classroom where this will be approved. If I take the kids to a store with these lights I prepare myself for a short stay in the store. The children can also have difficulties with moving lights and bright lights at amusement parks and carnivals.

Oral-motor Defensiveness

Oral-motor defensiveness (tactile defensiveness of the mouth) can cause difficulties with brushing teeth, getting rid of the baby bottle in a young child and difficulties with the child mouthing nonfood objects. Alex used to chew on his toys and put everything in his mouth. He ate the cover off of the box spring on his bed. Danielle chews crayons and did not give up her bottle until she was three years old. Adam has great difficulties with this. He puts everything in his mouth and eats anything he can find. He eats cardboard books, his wooden dressers, foam building blocks and raw meat out of the refrigerator. Children with this dysfunction also like to suck on toys, their fingers and even sometimes bite other children or themselves.

Olfactory Defensiveness

Olfactory defensiveness (intolerance to odors) is a reaction to certain smells. This can be from cleaning products used to clean a home or classroom, to food that is cooking. Some children cannot stand the smell of perfumes or hair spray. This can contribute to an autistic child not wanting to cooperate with a teacher or therapist. Alex cannot stand the smell of many cleaning products. I use a damp rag to dust the furniture in his room and the same laundry detergent all the time. I clean the bathroom when he isn't around and make sure the fan is on to get rid of the smell. Alex can smell food in the oven even when he is sleeping. It makes him hyper and sometimes he runs around the house uncontrollably.

One thing that always disturbs me is when a mother of a typical child says their child is just as active as my Alex, Danielle, Adam or Mitchell. A parent of a typical child cannot compare the activity level of their child to an autistic child. There are very distinct differences. Some of the characteristics of activity levels of autistic children are: disorganized and lacks purposeful play, uninvolved in the environment, lacks variety in play skills, poor balance and appears clumsy, difficulties calming and soothing self after becoming upset and the child seeks excessive amounts of vigorous sensory input.

An autistic child can have a short attention span and be *very* active. This child moves from one thing to another in a flash. The child is never satisfied with any one thing. The child goes through the room like a tornado. Even though the autistic child may pick up a toy and start to play with it, the child loses interest quickly and is distracted by the slightest thing. A typical active child may still play with a toy purposefully and manipulate the toy to figure out what it is all about. Alex never played with Legos correctly. He would dump them out and throw them around the room. Mitchell took a bucket full of army men and dumped them into one pile. He had no idea how to play with them and started lining them up in a straight, organized row. An autistic child lacks a purpose with an activity.

On the other hand an autistic child may have a long attention span and have great difficulty moving from one activity to the next. This is the opposite of a child with disorganized play skills. This child plays with a toy the same way over and over again. Danielle puts puzzles together for hours – one particular shape puzzle she puts together the same way every time. She puts in the blue circle than the green square then the red triangle, etc. She is very organized but lacks the ability to tolerate anything different. This long attention span causes a lack of variety in play skills.

I can remember people commenting what a "good" toddler Danielle was. When she was about two years old she was very content to stay in one place and never cried or complained about anything (as long as no one disturbed her). She was good tempered and very "easy going." As I learned of Danielle's diagnosis, I realized she lacked awareness of her environment and was living in "her own world." She had no desire to explore her environment or interact with those around her. Danielle would tune out noises including people talking to her. It seemed as though she was deaf. I remember being concerned about this and asking a pediatric psychologist if maybe Danielle was not stimulated enough because of having two older brothers with autism. The psychologist told me Danielle should be learning from her environment and wanting to explore the world around her, instead Danielle stayed to herself and needed to be forced to involve herself in her surroundings.

Balance and Coordination

An autistic child may have difficulties with balance and coordination. The child may fall forward without putting out their hands to stop themselves before they hit the ground. The child is impulsive and may do things that result in bruises, scratches or broken bones. Alex tripped outside on our driveway one time and fell right on his face. He did not put his hands out to stop himself and he had cuts, scrapes and bruises on his face as a result of this "non reaction" to falling Mitchell has very poor coordination. He cannot climb a ladder very well. He has difficulties with moving his hands and feet at the same time. Danielle has difficulties with coordination mainly because she runs through a room very fast with her head down and will run into walls, chairs or whatever is in her way. Adam climbs but is clumsy and will fall without landing on his feet. He walks on his toes and this makes him trip a lot. Most autistic children have poor gross motor skills that will improve with physical therapy, occupational therapy and sensory integration therapy.

All children enjoy spinning, jumping, swinging and wrestling but sometimes in an autistic child these activities can be excessive. The child may spin for long periods of time without becoming dizzy. Mitchell used to spin in the center of a room for almost thirty minutes. The child also may run into things on purpose or like things being thrown at them. Alex used to want Dan to throw a football to him. But instead of catching it he would let the ball hit his chest or face. Danielle and Adam love to be wrestled with and tackled hard. They also love being pushed in a swing for long periods of time.

Behaviors are usually the first indication of sensory dysfunction. The child may have frequent unexplained tantrums until it is understood the child is fearful of certain sounds, unable to tolerate certain smells and overwhelmed by certain visual stimuli. The child may have difficulties tolerating the feeling of certain clothing on their skin, and will strip clothes off and refuse to wear certain things. The child may become more active or hyper whenever there is a change in routine. I remember taking the kids up to my mother-in-law's house when they were very young. The kids would be skipping their naps and be outside most of the day. My mother-in-law would say, "They should be tired out for you tonight and should sleep well tonight." On the contrary, Alex and Mitchell would always be extra hyper and could not settle down to go to sleep. Dan and I couldn't understand why this happened until we read information on sensory dysfunction. Other obvious behaviors that describe sensory dysfunction are: a child screaming when someone hugs or touches them, a child not wanting to get dirty or on the other hand a child diving into mud and paint to feel it (this child has not a sensitive touch but a numb touch ability), a child screaming when her hair is shampooed, washed or cut, a child climbing up to high places and jumping, a child free falling down stairs or off of furniture and a child that screams or overreacts to certain sounds, smells and textures of food.

It is these behaviors, and others, that stem from sensory dysfunction that make autistic children so misunderstood and misjudged. Once the sensory dysfunction is identified, the behaviors can be controlled.

Sensory Integration Therapy

Sensory integration therapy is done by an occupational therapist that has specialized training in sensory integration. The best way to find a therapist who is most qualified is to call any hospital that treats children. These hospitals should be able to give names of clinics or hospitals that have occupational therapists who are qualified to work with sensory integration methods. The more training and experience, the better the therapist is capable of understanding what the child needs.

The therapists who are specialized in sensory integration do a variety of standardized tests and clinical observations to determine the problem areas and help to determine the best therapy needed. These therapists can help parents develop a sensory diet or sensory program for at home. They show parents how to identify when sensory methods should be used to help with child's hyper behavior, uncontrollable emotional behavior (continuous crying, the child does not know what they want, etc) and when it seems the child is seeking out sensory relief.

Sensory integration therapy is engaging the child in an activity which is very physical and fun, such as swinging in a net or on a board swing, wrapping the child in a mat or having the child jump from a platform onto a pile of big soft pillows. As the child is doing these activities, speech is encouraged. The child may be encouraged to count to ten and then jump, or say, "Ready, set, go!" before being swung on the swing, and so forth. The therapy is designed to help the child develop better sensory perception and have more control over their bodies. The therapy is to help organize all of the "sensory" information that their brains are absorbing from the environment.

A sensory integration activity, like swinging, is usually chosen by the child. Once the therapist sees the child enjoys and benefits from a certain physical activity, this activity is used for future sessions to entice the child to participate. During the sensory integration therapy session the child participates in a physical activity that also encourages speech, and then given an activity to do. For example, Mitchell may be swung in a net swing for six minutes then taken out of the swing to do a worksheet on numbers or letters. Once the worksheet is complete, the reward would be more physical sensory therapy. Then another activity is encouraged after so many minutes of the sensory physical activity. The therapy sessions can last as long as an hour, with an occupational therapist specialized in SI, a physical therapist and a speech therapist present.

Sensory integration therapists' goals include enhancing language, motor skills, attention span and limiting behaviors. A sensory integration therapy program should be developed for the autistic child in school as well as home. This will help the child be more attentive, less anxious and restless, and more willing to participate. The therapy is done in a room full of equipment that is very appealing to the autistic child. In most instances, sensory integration therapy is well liked by the autistic child. At school, the autistic child may have a place where sensory equipment is set up for when the sensory program is taking place. Some schools may not have the personnel or equipment to provide proper SI therapy. The topic should be brought to the school principal and board if a child needs the therapy though the school is not providing it. This should be investigated even before the child is enrolled into the school. In the meantime, the child should receive outside therapy from a clinic or hospital until the school is willing to provide what the child needs.

Sensory equipment is very expensive, and for the families to buy the equipment for home can be very difficult. The therapist should be able to develop a sensory program using inexpensive items that have similar effects as using the expensive equipment. For instance, Mitchell craves deep pressure. There are net swings and weighted blankets, vests and hats that cost between seventy and three hundred dollars apiece. Instead, we bought a heavy sleeping bag. Mitchell snuggles into it and it is heavy enough to give him the pressure he seeks. Alex benefits a lot from jumping. The sensory integration therapist uses a trampoline. Dan and I found an old mattress in the attic and let him jump on this. We even have him jump from a chair onto the mattress. Danielle loves swinging and spinning. We bought a tire swing and hung it from a tree in a neighbors' yard. This gives her the sensory input she needs. We even take her outside in the winter.

The sensory program developed for my four children focuses a lot around after school. I found the kids had a hard time transitioning from school to home. When Mitchell came home from school he would sometimes bury himself under his sleeping bag for hours. Alex would jump on his mattress or bury himself under blankets. Danielle liked to be held tight and adapted better once she felt one of us or her TSS held her. Adam liked to listen to music or watch a video with music. Summer time is great. Swimming is a big physical activity that helps the children with all of their sensory needs. Sometimes even a bath helps calm the kids and make them more attentive.

It took a long time for Dan and I to learn what helps at what time. We still are learning.

One of the most heartbreaking moments in my life was when a comment was made accusing me of not disciplining or controlling my children. It seems that professionals, family members and complete strangers feel compelled to tell me what they think about the way I am raising my children. I have to say that disciplining is the most difficult part of having autistic children. The behaviors have to be differentiated between sensory responses and defiance. Danielle went through a stage where she would take her pajamas off in her room. She would then urinate or have bowel movements in her bed and on the floor in her room. Dan and I dissected the whole behavior. What pajamas did she wear? What happened that day that was out of the ordinary? Did she nap too long? Did she crave the feeling of having nothing against her skin? Finally to avoid this behavior, we cut out her afternoon nap so that she would be very tired and fall right asleep when put to bed. We washed her new pajamas many times to prevent a different feeling from her clothes. And finally we kept her routine as structured as possible.

If a typical child would have done this, the parent could have given the child consequences for those actions, and the child would be able to connect the behavior with the consequence. This is difficult for autistic children to do. So my disciplining is quite different. When Danielle smeared feces across her carpet, part of my disciplining was to have her help me scrub the carpet. This was hands on learning, by her, that if she does this again she will have to clean this up again with mom, and it was very effective. Alex used to pull all his clothes out of his dresser drawers and throw them around the room. I used to discipline him by having him help me pick them up. This behavior soon ended. If Mitchell would shove his younger brother Adam, Dan and I would make him sit in a chair with a visual timer for six minutes and make him go over to Adam and say "I am sorry" (which Mitchell can do because he is more verbal). These actions that consistently follow a behavior do help to curb the undesirable behavior. The hardest part about disciplining, though, is knowing when a behavior is due to a sensory dysfunction problem or just bad behavior. For example, Mitchell would sit on the floor at school with his hands over his ears when the students all said the Pledge of Allegiance to the flag. At first, the teacher assumed he just did not want to participate and was being uncooperative. Then when a sensory integration therapist assessed the room, he felt the response was sensory. The solution: Mitchell did not arrive in the kindergarten classroom until the Pledge of Allegiance of the flag was said. He was taken up to the gym where he was swung for ten minutes before class. This did keep him calm and cooperative the rest of the morning. Also, Alex would spit milk or juice all over the family room at times. Dan and I thought he was just being bad at first until we told this behavior to his sensory integration therapist. He said it was an oral sensory response because Alex was craving oral stimulation. Alex has a lot of sensory difficulties (more than my other children). The solution was to have him blow bubbles, drink out of a straw or chew gum. This worked tremendously. In fact, Dan and I can tell when he needs to do an oral activity. Danielle splashes uncontrollably in the bathtub. She gets everything wet. After reading a book on sensory integration, I learned this is a tactile sensory need for her. She craves the water and feeling the water. This also calms her. The solution: we pull a shower curtain around the tub when she gets a bath and we bath her last. We give her some time to splash before we bath her. This works too.

Sensory integration methods are not accepted by all professionals, but I know first hand the methods have helped me a great deal. My goals as a parent of autistic children are not the same as parents who have typical children, and this makes it easy for others to pass judgment on my parenting skills. But what people don't realize is that all of us have the responsibility as parents to raise our children the best we can and that is all I am trying to do, with a lot more challenges than most people.

Self-stimulatory Behavior

Self-stimulatory behavior refers to repetitive body movements or repetitive movements of an object. It is very common in autism. Individuals who are not diagnosed with autism and have self-stimulatory behaviors are often labeled to have autistic tendencies or characteristics. These behaviors arouse the five senses. Some examples are staring at lights, moving fingers in front of ones eyes or face repeatedly, hand flapping, tapping ears, making vocal sounds like grunting, humming and repeating phrases over and over, scratching or rubbing an object continuously, licking objects, putting objects in ones mouth, rocking back and forth or side to side, moving ones hand or arm in a jerky movement, smelling objects, smelling people, banging the side of ones head with a closed fist, spinning oneself, running in circles, inappropriate jumping and clapping. Other forms of self-stimulatory behavior are obsessions with rituals or routines. Such as lining objects up in an organized row and holding items in ones hands all the time. Sensory overload triggers the self-stimulatory behaviors. Sensory overload is when an autistic person is overwhelmed with their environment. The self-stimulatory behaviors help the autistic child calm down, shut out overwhelming noise and reduce stress in uncomfortable situations. In other words there is too much going on in the environment around them and they seek a way to block out all of the confusion, distraction and unsafe feelings.

These behaviors are not easily extinguished and many therapists work at this as a goal. Sometimes, though, if an autistic child is in sensory overload due to their environment, the child may lessen self-stimulatory behaviors when removed from the environment and given some sensory integration therapy. Self-stimulatory behaviors can be allowed in certain places at certain times. An autistic individual can learn to control them in certain situations like grocery stores, in church, at school, etc. with much teaching. An autistic person can be prepared for a situation that may trigger a self-stimulatory response such as change in routine, a busy, fast moving environment or an uncomfortable situation.

My children have self-stimulatory behaviors but the behaviors have changed a great deal as the children have grown and matured. Mitchell used to cross his eyes, spin in circles and run in circles around the house for great lengths of time. It broke my heart to see him hit his head with his fists and rock back and forth at his kindergarten orientation test. I was glad when the test was finished. Mitchell likes everything to be perfect – no broken cookies, everything matching, no puzzle pieces missing, etc. Alex grunts, hums and talks very loudly all the time. He runs in circles around the house and needs to have gum in his mouth, blow bubbles, drink from a straw for oral sensory cravings. He has eaten and licked toys. Alex even puts a pacifier in his mouth at times to ease the cravings. This self-stimulatory behavior is seen mostly when he is very tired, bored and overwhelmed. Danielle does a lot of jumping and clapping, moving her hands in front of her face, holding objects continuously in her hands, picking her nose and crossing her eyes. She does these behaviors a lot when she is excited or happy, bored and very angry. Danielle is good at blocking out her environment anyway, but she is slowly starting to be more aware. Adam jumps up and down in place, flaps his hands, spins anything he can find and loves to watch this move (he will get really close to the television set and move his head as things move on the screen).

This chapter on sensory integration therapy is only a pebble in comparison to the information that is available in books and on the Internet. My mission was not to explain the clinical aspects of sensory integration therapy but to explain that these sensory needs and dysfunctions affect an autistic child's behavior, and that the autistic child should not be judged for their behaviors alone. There are reasons behind many behaviors that need to be explored and understood. Sensory information should be shared with all who are involved with the autistic child, especially teachers, principals and school aids. The better it is understood the more patience, understanding and compassion will be shown to the child. Unfortunately, in schools, the autistic child is often marked as a behavioral problem before the child even starts the school year. Many people identify autism with violence, aggression and overall bad behavior. This is a generalization and not factual. Each autistic child is different, just like each typical child is different. The sensory dysfunction gives the autistic child extra challenges to face everyday. These challenges need to be identified, the environment modified (possibly) and those involved with the child need to be patient.

ಎಂಚ

Chapter 9
Safety and Security Measures

In the process of writing this book, a horrific story about a nine-year-old, autistic boy who became lost substantiated my worst fears of what can happen all too easily. Dan and I watched in horror as the news reporter explained that the child had gotten out of his house and his family could not find him. A search team with search dogs was deployed into subfreezing, single-digit temperatures. The boy did not talk nor respond to his name when being called. His parents had to teach the police, search team and volunteers about autism so they knew how to find him. Sadly, the boy was found under a tree three days later; he lost his life to malnutrition and hypothermia. Dan and I were simply sick over what had happened.

No one can rightfully place blame on anyone for what happened to this boy. But seeing the need for these parents to have to explain autistic traits to municipal personnel made me all the more determined to bring up the awareness and understanding levels of autism. Experts in autism may likely not have found this boy any sooner. Still, I feel *strongly* that police, firemen, paramedics and other similar municipal personnel should be trained on the basics of autism and how to handle autistic children if only because they should know this information to potentially save a life in the future. Though we were almost done with the writing process of this book, I decided to go back and include this chapter in order to enlighten as many people as possible. I hope and pray that this book, and this chapter, might help with this. This chapter is dedicated to the nine year old boy and his loving family.

Preventative Measures

Autistic children have a tendency to be very impulsive, and their awareness of what is dangerous and what is safe is lacking. An autistic child, for instance, will dart into the street without even looking, grab a pot of boiling water on the stove without hesitation and dart off or wander away without realizing the danger of getting too far away from what is familiar, ultimately becoming lost.

Safety First!

Mitchell once put a straw down his throat, put a plastic bag over his head and tied a string from a toy around his neck. Alex has been on the roof, ate the cover off of his box spring to his bed and choked on it. (We could hear him gagging on the monitor and went up to see what happened. This was before we had the camera system in the bedroom upstairs.) He also cut the top of his finger off in a door at the local YMCA. Danielle has followed Dan out the door without him knowing it, jumped down a large number of non-carpeted steps and has spilled a pot of boiling water from the stove on herself. Adam has pinched his fingers in the hinge of a door, choked on a small wooden toy and has knocked the television down on himself. The list goes on forever.

There are measures that can be taken for preventing autistic child from becoming lost or injured. Of course, the common child safety rules of any home should be used:

- Turn pot handles inward when cooking, away from a child's reach.

- Keep any potentially dangerous items such as knives and other sharp items out of reach.

- Put away any potential choking items.

- Lock up household cleaning supplies.

- Keep medicines out of reach.

- Lock up garbage bags and throw away plastic bags for dry cleaning.

- Do not purchase toys with small parts even if the autistic child is older. Autistic children have a tendency of putting anything in their mouths.

- Keep doors and windows locked at all times.

- Secure screens or put window guards on windows to prevent the child from pushing out a screen.

- Do not give an autistic child glass plates or bowls to eat from.

- Put gates or doors up that lead into the kitchen and do not let the children in there when you are cooking. Even if an autistic child gets burned once, they still may be fascinated with what is on the stove or in the oven.

- Monitor whether the autistic child should sleep on a bed and frame or if the child should simply have a mattress set on the floor. My children all have mattresses on the floor because they have jumped up and down on their beds and fell off, consequently needing stitches.

- Secure dressers, standing cabinets, televisions, etc., such that if the child climbs or pulls on the items, they will not fall on top of them.

- Put a fence around the yard if you live on a busy road.

- Look into putting a sign in front of your house that says, "Watch Children," "Caution Deaf Child," or anything that could warn traffic if your child has a tendency to dart across the street, EVEN IF IT IS NOT A BUSY STREET.

- Keep all tools locked up.

This is a start, but greater measures are required for autistic children. Autistic children do not know even the simplest ways to keep themselves safe. They are fearless and oblivious to danger.

Lock It Up
Children are good climbers. Things considered "out of reach" can likely, one day, become "within reach." Medicine in the medicine cabinet is insufficient and needs to be locked away as well as any other potential hazards. Doors and drawers are no defense for the curious autistic child at any age. And just because they have been told a hundred times before that something is dangerous, there is absolutely no reason to think that they will stay clear of these hazards, they won't. Play it safe and lock it up.

Alex climbed up on our dishwasher and then onto the

refrigerator last Christmas and carried down a butcher knife (we kept the knives in a sealed Tupperware container on top of the refrigerator at that time) and preceded to cut a rubber ball we bought him for Christmas. I was in the bathroom and Dan was in the living room at the time this happened. It happened in a split second. Dan walked into the family room and found Alex with the knife and the other young children ran into the room at that very same moment. No one got hurt. Dan and I had nightmares about the incident for months afterwards.

Security Measures

Many autistic children are exceptional escape artists. They are very good at getting out of the house and fenced yard when they're not supposed to. A loose fence board or a gap between posts that seemingly a hamster couldn't get through, a gate left unlocked or access to a bolt positioned eight feet high are no match for the child. These are just a few examples of how it is very difficult to create a foolproof dwelling. There are security measures you can take in securing your home and yard and keeping your child safe.

Breaching the Dwelling

Alex has gotten out of the house many times. He has gone out windows, doors and scaled our six-foot fence in our backyard. The alarm system goes off each time but by the time it sounds, he is already gone within seconds. He bolts from the dwelling. Alex has picked open every lock we've had so far that has secured our windows and doors. He's disassembled many different alarm systems too.

Autistic children can be very determined to get their own way and will leave the house or yard because of something they may have seen somewhere else earlier that day or week. Please remember the child is not being manipulative or "bad." An autistic child has a tendency to be very focused on what they want and do not understand the consequences of their actions nor do they totally understand what is in the world around them. Alex likes to throw stones down sewer drains. When he got out of our house for the first time this is where he was found - throwing rocks down a sewer drain. To him, this was fascinating. I don't know why and may never understand it.

Autistic children explore the world differently than we do and at a different pace. I may notice something every time I walk down the block but one of my autistic children may not notice it until five or six times walking down that same block. Each child is different and each has different levels of impulsiveness, curiosity and insight into the world.

Locks and Bolts

Dan and I have tried combination locks, locks with keys and simple hook locks on our doors. We place the locks high on our doors. We have put screws securely into the frames of our windows such that they can only open slightly and a person cannot climb out of them. The lock and key is used very infrequently and only if Dan and I are having great difficulties with Alex that day. Having a key and lock, for me, is frightening because what if there were to be a fire in the home? The combination lock works well, but Alex has memorized the combination of numbers and has figured out how to open these kinds of locks. Alex is also a very skilled climber and can unhook hook locks quite well. Dan and I have secured things as best as possible and have to the point of double-locking, or setting an alarm to almost everything.

All of the children have locks on the outside of their bedroom doors. They are locked into their bedrooms at night because the thought of any of them wandering around the house at night unsupervised is scary.

Window and Door Alarms

There are alarms you can purchase that go off when windows or doors are opened. This can give some warning to your child getting out when he/she is not supposed to. The alarms can sound when the door or window opens.

There are also alarms that can be installed under carpets to sound when the child approaches a door or window. There are alarms that are placed inside windows to sound when the window is even touched as well as alarms that sound when the window is open. We have air conditioning in our home because it is unsafe for us to keep the windows open due to Alex's obsession for climbing out of them. Alex even disassembles the window guards. For him, being outside is a goal, and he will do what it takes to meet this goal.

Deter Wandering

It can take but a brief moment to lose track of your child in a crowded environment. Often, calling out their name will be completely ignored and each passing second can take the child further from you.

Here are a few ideas for keeping your child close and safe:

Child Distance Alarms

There are two-piece, wireless alarm systems that sound on the parent's unit when the child moves beyond a certain distance. The child holds the transmitter (usually can be strapped to their waist) and the parent/guardian holds on to the receiver unit. These are practical for crowded conditions such as when shopping, at a parade or festival and so forth.

Some alarm systems are not practical. For instance, a loud alarm or siren from the child's unit could cause the child to become hysterical and possibly cause greater danger to himself through his reaction to the sound.

You can type "CHILD ALARMS" on the Internet search engines such as Yahoo or Google to find companies with these types of products.

Identification Bracelets and Wristbands

Identification bracelets are a big help for a child that does not or will not speak to strangers. They are effective if someone finds your child. The bracelet displays a telephone number that the good Samaritan can call.

There are different kinds of bracelets from metal to nylon-Velcro styles. And if you can't get your child to keep one on their wrist, there are shoe fasteners that can go around the laces.

Type "CHILD BRACELETS" at the search engines.

MedicAlert:

www.medicalert.org/Main/KidSmartAutism.aspx
offers a membership and bracelet which allows people, who find the child, to call the number on the bracelet.

High Tech Tracking Devices

There are more sophisticated ways to track your child using GPS (Global Positioning System). GPS uses satellites to track precise locations on the planet.

One company has a watch-like, personal locator that enables you to locate your child's position to within a few feet of accuracy. Parents can either call a toll-free number or go on-line (the Internet) and type in their user ID and private security code. They are able to see a map with the closest street addresses where the lost child is located.

Go to: www.wherifywireless.com/prod_watches.htm

This one tracks up to four kids:

www.brickhouse security.com/vbsik.html

Type "SATELLITE CHILD MONITORS" at the search engines for more GPS products.

Though Dan and I do all that we can think of to keep our kids safe and sound, Alex is the one I worry about most because he's the escape artist and wanderer. His behavior approaches the most danger of all my kids. He still finds ways to get out of the house or yard.

The precaution options listed in this chapter are not all of the ways you can protect your autistic child. And no matter what protection you decide to use, never become lax because precautious measures have been taken. Don't "assume" that your child is tucked away safely. Check on him/her as much as before. An autistic child may not keep any sort of alarm on their bodies either. This can make things even more tricky.

Escaping from the home at any time of the day or night can bring untold hazards. Alarm systems, locks high on doors, window guards and locks on windows, a surveillance system in your home, a fence around the yard, a handicap sign on the vehicle so you can park in the front of the parking lot or even the watchful eye of a trained dog can be used to prevent a tragedy but sometimes this is still not enough.

The potential for an autistic child to escape a home or wander away also makes it very difficult to go to another person's house to visit or stay. Dan and I have to have a plan before we visit anyone else's house. We do not underestimate the autistic child's ability to get lost in unfamiliar surroundings. The thought of one of my children wandering away at a picnic or family function scares me a lot. Therefore, we attend very few parties or gatherings unless we have security measures in place. Most of the time, family members will say to us, "I will help you 'watch' the kids." But one does not "watch" autistic children; it requires constant hands-on supervision. The child cannot ever be out of sight. And others, who do not know the autistic child, do not really know how to supervise them safely, at least not without detailed and proper instruction. But, in most cases, even that falls short of being prepared to deal with an autistic child. Anything short of proper training can be very dangerous.

Searching for an Autistic Child

As the frequency of lost autistic children has increased with autism's growth over the past decade, it is becoming more essential for emergency personnel to better understand autism.

An autistic child getting out of the house or wandering away is a nightmare for all involved, including the emergency personnel. In most cases, the child does not speak well and is therefore unable to say his name, address, phone number, mother's name, father's name, etc. The child will typically not come when called due to poor receptive speech and understanding. Emergency personnel must physically look for the child and utilize as many searchers as possible to help.

Planning and coordination is key to a swift, positive outcome if your child were ever to show up missing. Here are a few things you can do as a precaution.

1. **Reach out to your neighbors and let them know about your child.** You could have cards or fliers made up with your telephone number(s) and anything you want them to understand about your child as well as what to do if they were to find your child wandering alone.

Things such as how to approach the child, what to say or not say, any specifics should be stated. Don't assume they will know what to do, leave nothing out that you feel they should know or do. They will appreciate this information if ever needed and will handle the situation like you would, which can give you some peace of mind as well.

2. As a precautionary measure, bring a picture of your child to the police station. Finger prints are a good idea as well, which you can typically get done while at the station if you bring your child along. You can include any relevant things you feel police should know about your child. These things will be on file and may save time if your child should become lost in the future.

When searching for an autistic child who is missing, here are some suggestions:

1. Alert neighbors and anyone in the vicinity that the autistic child is missing.

2. Brief them on what they should do if they see the child.

   If my Alex gets out of the house, some of my neighbors go to different likely places in the neighborhood that he might go to, some come with the kids and me.

3. When parents call emergency personnel, it is important for them to know that there is an autistic child involved. Make sure they know this. Give them

a description of the child's clothing and distinct features (height, weight, hair color, etc.). Let them know whether your child speaks or not and what he/she would respond to if they were to encounter the child- a favorite truck, action figure, book, piece of clothing, a family photo, etc.

4. When the child wanders away or is missing, the parents need to give a list of places they feel their child may be or may visit, especially places where the child has been to recently. Also give a list of the child's hobbies or favorite things to do like swimming, bike riding, reading, etc. This may help narrow down the places to look.

5. Remember the child does not have any safety awareness and will jump in streams, ponds and pools, will dart in front of traffic, eat out of garbage, etc. The emergency personnel must look in others' garages, in sheds, under porches, under a pile of leaves, even in dumpsters. The child may hide if scared or seek out some sensory input due to the realization that they do not know where they are. This means the child may bury himself under leaves or hide in a small, tight place or jump on a trampoline or be interested in the movement of objects.

6. The child will not seek out help by knocking on windows or doors of other homes or by flagging a car down on the street. The child is unaware of how to get others' attention for help.

7. Sometimes the media can be a big help. A radio station may even agree to mention about the missing child and give the child's description. This could help

a great deal.

A parent, or someone the child can recognize, should be included in the physical search just in case the child may be too scared to go with a policeman or an emergency personnel (the child may also run the opposite way). If the child is hiding in a place where it may be difficult to see him/her, a familiar face may cause the child to come out. Only the parent knows the child completely and can predict how the they will react to the situation. I know my Alex if he was hiding may come out for my husband if he saw him or maybe heard his voice but yet Alex only responds to his name about 25% of the time. It is a very unpredictable situation.

An autistic child also does not know how to predict danger and may go with anyone. Even if this person is someone who does not have good intentions. One very scary thing for a parent of an autistic child is the fact that a child with autism cannot be taught to stay away from strangers and due to poor communication skills can't inform others if someone hurts them. This means when a child wanders away from home the thought of someone taking the child is a very possible one, especially if he/she wanders onto a highway or in someone's yard. The police should knock on neighbors' doors and ask many questions of people in the surrounding areas when the child is missing. Especially if they are a known child molester. Also, someone may have seen the child with someone else and may help prevent a tragedy from happening by describing to the police what they saw.

In Times of Injury

Emergency personnel are not only involved when the child is missing. They can also be involved when an autistic child is injured or in times of a house fire. When an autistic child falls and breaks their arm or hurts themselves in any way, the emergency personnel's reaction and handling of the child's disability is very important. The child is more afraid and can be in more pain due to sensory sensitivities than a typical child. The child may hit, kick, thrash, scream, cry and so forth, for a very long period of time. Talking calmly and softly to the child will help even though the child may be unable to process all that is being said. Singing a song or having a family member present with the child no matter what (even if a parent is not normally allowed with the child) will make a big difference. Screaming at the child, restraining the child (unnecessarily of course, sometimes it is necessary), not telling him/her what you are doing or having too many people attending to the child at one time can make them scream, kick, hit, bite and more.

With autism increasing as much as it has, it is vital that emergency personnel learn more about autism. Hopefully, many will read this book. Autistic children require extra care and understanding during trying times and times of need. If we do all we can, as parents, as a family and as a community, autistic children everywhere will live safer lives.

ಐೂ

Chapter 10
Other Challenges

The parents of autistic children are continually faced with new challenges, never knowing what might arise next. Overcoming these obstacles can take an abundance of time and energy. By the end of each week I am physically, emotionally and mentally drained as autism consumes my every action and decision made.

My mission in this chapter is to explain other challenges that parents face. Each challenge in itself may seem small, but combined, the mountain to climb can become daunting. Coming to understand these aspects better can help wane the incline to a more palatable stride.

Financial Burden

Therapy for an autistic child is on-going and lifelong, and so too are the medical expenses. Dan and I took Mitchell and Alex to sensory integration therapy in Pittsburgh, PA for 10 months. This trip was an exhausting 3 hours one way.

They needed the therapy very badly. Mitchell finally starting to print his name as a result—something many occupational therapists told me he would never do. Alex began to give more spontaneous speech as well.

The therapy was not covered entirely by our primary insurance and the therapy organization did not accept the medical assistance card (more on this card later). We paid for the therapy as we could each week. Finally, after the kids attended this facility for 10 months, the therapy organization told us we could not come back unless we paid the outstanding balance and could pay the full amount each week. The therapy at that time was $420.00 per week and we had an outstanding balance of approximately $2,000.00. Dan and I were very angry and frustrated; we wanted our children to get the therapy they so very much needed. After much searching, we found another place that would take our children for this therapy. Though business is business we, as parents have never forgotten the pain it caused us to see people be so uncaring towards our children. But as the problem is not any particular therapy organization as they have bills to pay just as well, it lies more so in the gaps in coverage to support the autistic.

Primary insurance like HMOs and Blue Cross/Blue Shield do not cover autism as a diagnosis though it is covered under category PS 95, which is a special assistance rule known as the "loophole." This is often helpful as it allows children with autism to receive the medical assistance card regardless of family income. This insurance can pay for doctor appointments, therapy and wraparound services. But unfortunately, even with the existence of the medical assistance card, there are circumstances that can create outstanding medical expenses to burden the family which can pile up over time.

For one thing, there are many places that do not accept the medical assistance card. And parents are often left with the dilemma of whether they can afford to take their child for needed medical and therapeutic treatment or to conclude that they just cannot afford them. Typically, the decision is to put the child first and "do it anyway," then figure out how to pay the bills later.

Autism affects family finances in other ways as well. The cost for babysitting is much higher for an autistic child. We have to pay a babysitter a higher rate to watch our children, due to their many challenges, while Dan and I go to work. There are difficulties with toilet training, the continual expense of purchasing pull-ups, new blankets, sheets and pillows adds up quickly. Dan and I have to take off work, at times without pay, to take care of them on their "bad" days. This is yet another financial burden of lost wages.

Our solution, though not all encompassing, is to work many odd jobs to pay for these types of expenses. We, as in all parents of autistic children, want so badly to give our children every opportunity to succeed. The many videos, computer games, CDs and books that can help with speech and following directions are costly. The special summer camps that help autistic children with social awkwardness designed specifically for helping special needs children to make friends are also very expensive. Sensory equipment, even when cutting corners, is costly too.

Dan and I also have a yard sale every summer and with this money, we buy things that the kids need. Our neighbors pitch in items for us to sell. Every child is expensive but the autistic child's needs are so much greater that sometimes the parents have to choose between sacrificing what their child so desperately needs because the cost is simply too great. This brings a lot of guilt, feelings of failure, inadequacy and sadness upon the parents. The challenge of financial hardship, I think, is the most difficult to overcome.

Finding a Babysitter

Finding a babysitter who will watch more than one autistic child is nearly impossible. Dan and I have one sitter who comes to the house in the morning. She stays six hours watching my other children, while Dan sleeps. He works the night shift and I work day shift. During these six hours Mitchell, Alex, Adam and Danielle are in school unless it is summer or with their TSS worker. The day is purposely planned this way. There is no way one babysitter can handle the many challenges of four autistic children and three typical children (we have seven children total) by herself without some help. Dan and I make it as easy as possible for the babysitter but there still are many difficulties and challenges she faces daily that she would not face with typical children.

For example, difficulties with toilet training, complexities with understanding what they want due to poor expressive speech, the children's inability to follow directions or come when called, the sensory needs and high activity levels when these needs are not being met, the potential for the children to escape from the home unattended, their inconsistent eating habits and ritualistic daily routines that are so very much required and the list goes on and on. Our current sitter, Adrian, was trained with Dan and I for one month before she was left alone with the kids. She has become part of their routine and the kids are not upset with me when I leave for work every day. This is a wonderful feeling.

Though the babysitting routine is great for our work schedules, it becomes very difficult if Dan and I have to go out to do something otherwise. We don't try to do too many things and be gone long because the kids need to be with someone who knows them and understands their needs. Although Adrian does baby sit for us at night on occasion, she needs a break just as well. Dan and I can't just leave the kids with anyone. The person needs to be with the kids for a while to understand their needs and the kids need to feel comfortable with the person if Dan and I are not there. Anyone babysitting our children needs to be on constant guard that one or more of the children could leave the home unattended. We have high locks on the doors, one or two locks on every window, an alarm system in the home and a camera system in the upstairs bedrooms all to help keep the children in the home and prevent a tragedy from happening. This is one of the most significant reasons why we cannot take the children anywhere else to be watched; most other homes do not have these security measures in place. Babysitting our children requires constant supervision, anticipating their every move. And this is difficult to ask of someone.

If we were to have someone to baby sit who the kids didn't know, they may not sleep or eat, or could become so active it that would become very difficult to calm them down. The babysitter would also become frustrated and the experience would not be a good one for all concerned. And this would come back to haunt us as the kids would feel insecure if we tried to leave them again.

Dan and I have found ways to get out for some alone time even though babysitters are hard to come by. We go to breakfast at least three times a month. I also take vacation days; Dan skips some of his sleep for the night shift and we go shopping for the day. Or we plan ahead and give Adrian a weekday off to come on a Saturday morning instead as a tradeoff. We've even gone out after the kids have gone to bed for a late movie - with Adrian there of course.

There have been many family holiday dinners, neighborhood parties and work functions Dan and I have missed. I do not regret any of it. I simply wish that people were more understanding as to why we might not accept an invitation, and not take it personally or feel that we are antisocial or even worse, that we simply do not like them. Dropping off my kids at the in-laws or calling an alternative neighborhood teenager to baby sit at the last minute if Adrian can't watch them is simply not an option for us. Things are not that easy when you have autistic children. We have lost friends and upset people simply because autism, and how it affects the lives it touches, is not understood. I have hopes this book will help with this issue for all parents of autistic children.

Administrational Responsibilities

One challenge for me is all the paperwork involved with having four autistic children. Mitchell, Alex, Danielle and Adam have notebooks for school that the TSS workers, teachers, therapists and Dan and I write in. This book helps his TSS and teacher with any problems that may arise at home which could affect how he interacts in school that day. For example, if Mitchell did not sleep well the night before or I gave him some cold medicine that might make him drowsy, I would write this in his notebook. This way it wouldn't be misconstrued that the child has regressed.

The teacher and aid write notes every day as well, describing how their day went. This correspondence helps me, the teacher and his TSS better predict the children's mood and sensory needs in school and after they get home. Alex has the waiver program which provides some money to help with expenses. The waiver program requires papers to be filled out by the pediatrician and the babysitter - Adrian. It is my responsibility to make sure the papers are filled out and faxed to the waiver program on time. Writing in four notebooks daily is time consuming as well as sending in yearly renewal applications for medical assistance, at least once per month signing and reading IEPs and providing documentation for mandatory meetings in proving the need for wraparound services as well as filling out paperwork for case management quarterly and so on. This paperwork and completing the papers sent home from school is very tedious and time consuming. I often joke with Dan that I need a secretary!

Preparing for the Holidays

Holidays are a time when families get together to be thankful for each other and the time they have to spend with each other when an otherwise demanding world denies such privileges. Parents of autistic children have challenges with holidays that other people are not always aware of. Dan and I are prepared to have difficult days when the kids are off from school for the holidays. Autistic children do not adapt well to changes in their routines, as I have already mentioned, and the biggest change in routine is when school is not in session. Alex, Mitchell, Adam and Danielle are very active and especially hyper when there is no school. Some say they are bored, others assert it is because there is too much time on their hands and still others conjure it is an anxiety over not knowing what to expect. I usually have wraparound services come as much as they can when there is a holiday vacation from school. This helps fill in some of the time.

Along with the changes from the absence of school, the holidays bring their own challenges. There are more people in the home, usually visiting relatives. This is more change and it is very difficult for the children. Alex usually does not sleep well from Thanksgiving until after Christmas. He can tell there is something different. Not only is there a Thanksgiving and Christmas break from school, my schedule changes which does not go unnoticed. I bake cookies, wrap gifts, leave more often to go shopping and there is the Christmas tree, Christmas lights and Santa decorations - all a change from the norm. Dan and I have learned to put up the tree one day, decorate the next and then let the kids be involved in making decorations to put on the tree. This helps our autistic children adapt to the tree being there. The very presence of the tree is a change and brings about a series of behaviors and uncertainty for them. The Fourth of July and Memorial Day are also difficult because of the fire works, parades and large picnics.

The autistic child needs to be prepared for the holidays and the parents need to be open minded to what difficulties the holidays might impose. Dan and I do not take the children anywhere on Christmas Day and Thanksgiving. It is just too much. People do come and visit us and this seems to work best for my children. Dan and I have as many holidays and gatherings at our house as we can. This helps lessen the strain. Taking the kids to another house and dealing with crowds is usually too much to handle for everyone concerned. One year we took the kids to Dan's aunt's house for Christmas Eve, Alex went to the door with his shoes and coat. He wanted to go outside and would not come in to face the crowd of people in the house. Dan and I do push the kids a little but we always take their signals when they have had enough. Alex bringing us his shoes and coat meant he had reached his limit and needed to leave. Danielle crying and running around trying to get away from everyone is a signal we have to leave as well. Mitchell spinning in circles or whining without reason means this as well. Adam, when he needs to leave a situation, will pull on my pant leg and whine. Sometimes Adam will even hide behind a chair or couch. My mom always has a buffet style dinner because sitting down for dinner at a big table with lots of people is too difficult for Mitchell, Alex, Adam and Danielle. I am a ball of nerves before the holidays because I try to please all of the relatives and hope they understand why our family cannot visit sometimes or why we leave early all of the time.

Holidays bring change in routine, new experiences and crowds - all of which are intolerable to the autistic child. All a parent can do is learn how to make the child feel as comfortable as possible and try to create a pleasant and happy holiday as possible. Dan and I try to make each holiday special for the kids, no matter what we have to do.

Acceptance from other Parents and Peers

All parents want their children to have friends. Autistic children have great difficulties with social situations, therefore making friends is an enormous challenge. Typically, children will label autistics as "nerdy," "odd" or "weird" to their peers because of their ritualistic (habitual) tendencies, poor communication skills and an inability to understand proper social etiquette. The thought of my children being made fun of because they are "different" just tears my heart out.

In August of 2003, I took Danielle to her orientation for "regular" preschool, Alex to his orientation for "regular" preschool and Mitchell to his kindergarten orientation all on the same day at different times. They each had aids with them and the teachers introduced my children and the aids. At that moment I could see the preconceived opinions and condemning judgments in the other children's' eyes and on their parents' faces. One parent asked the teacher after I had left with Alex if Alex would be crying all the time in school like he had that particular day when everyone made him feel different and not accepted. That day, after I came home from the last orientation, I closed the front door and began to weep. I told Dan I wished I could lock all the doors and windows and let no one in or out. I wish I could protect our children from the cruel, judgmental, "need to be just like me" world which we live in. After this experience, I was certain I did not want to put Adam through the same hardships of regular preschool. I chose to put him in special education preschool, took him to outpatient therapy once a week and had him spend one-on-one time with a TSS doing things with Adam in the community with the goal that he would improve his social awkwardness. This seems to be working and Adam is thriving. Dan and I do the best we can to instill self-confidence in our children. We also have been bringing them into social situations slowly to help them make some friends and be accepted. We have introduced them to swimming lessons, T-ball, gymnastics and the movie theaters. My goal is to develop a social group or group of typical children my kids' age to come over and play. This could be very educational to other children and their parents, and may give my children the self-confidence they need to feel accepted and make friends on their own.

Toilet Training

Toilet training is very difficult for any special needs child. Because it involves the development of many different behavioral and physical abilities that are controlled by certain brain centers, a developmental delay affecting any of these areas can affect the special needs child's toileting abilities. The poor ability to communicate, resistance to change (different bathrooms in different places), poor attention span and a lack of body awareness all play a part in why toileting skills are so challenging. Lacking body awareness is the inability of the child to know how to read ones own body, whether it be pain or the urge to go to the bathroom. Mitchell may complain of a headache when, in fact, it is his stomach that really hurts. He needs to be told when to use the bathroom. He does not have the awareness to connect the feeling of needing to go to the bathroom with the actual act. At seven years of age, he still has accidents.

The autistic child can also have set backs with toileting

skills from schedule changes mentioned earlier such as when school is out for vacations, during holidays, the birth of a new sibling or any change in routine as well as having to get used to too many different bathrooms at one time (school, home, the babysitter's, etc.) Alex will have great toileting skills for months and then one little change will make him scream and cry whenever he has to enter the bathroom. This is so discouraging for a parent. The poor and inconsistent toileting skills make it difficult for the child to go to birthday parties, stay over night at grandmother's house and make friends in school.

Some special needs children do have physical problems that require medical attention to monitor the situation, but most will have toileting issues until the age of eight or nine. This is a long road but with some patience and flexibility on the parent's behalf the autistic child will get through this difficult time.

On Religion

Religion has been a big part of my life since I can remember. In fact, one of my dreams when my first child, Mitchell, was born was to be able to teach him about the strength found in prayer and the deep inner faith in God. When Mitchell, Adam Danielle and Alex were diagnosed with autism, I was puzzled how I could get my children who have difficulties with the abstract to understand God and prayer. Dan and I take the children to church when it is empty and show them the cross, the alter, the holy water and the statues of Jesus and Mary. We are starting with the basics and building on what they seem to understand. Mitchell knows the statue is Jesus but does not understand how the statue inside the church is Jesus and the statue outside the church is Jesus, too. Mitchell is a literal thinker so to him the statue *is* Jesus not a symbol of Jesus. Alex understands he needs to be quite in church but continues to blow out the candles on the alter. Teaching religious practices, the meaning of religious holidays and reciting prayers are difficult for my children. It is much harder for my children to understand the abstract concepts and recite the common prayers (due to poor speech and comprehension) than typical children. It is also more difficult for Dan and I to get our children to behave properly in church. Besides having difficulties comprehending the information being recited, there are a lot of people reciting aloud (auditory defensiveness) and the amount of people present in the church presents some discomfort for the autistic child.

Slowly introducing more and more about God, prayer and establishing comfort with the interactions of going to church as the children can have it, is the best practice for teaching our autistic children of their religion.

Repetition of Commands

The term "sounds like a broken record" describes Dan's and my day exactly. Difficulties following directions involves continuous repetition of instructions, warnings and disciplining the same issue over and over again, sometimes many times in just a single hour. The phrase, "I get tired of hearing myself talk" fits as well by the end of each day. Mitchell needs step-by-step instructions on how to get dressed the same way day after day. Alex and Adam love to climb. Alex can climb the bookcase to change a VCR tape at least five times in the first fifteen minutes he is awake each morning. Adam will climb up the on the back of the couch and take pictures off of the wall. I give them both the same instruction daily: "Get down Alex or Adam." Danielle steals her brothers' breakfast every day if they don't eat fast enough. Each day I solve the problem of her stealing someone else's breakfast and try to calm her down when I take the plate from her and give it back to her brother. I have to say to her "This is not yours Danielle."

The continuous repeating of words becomes exhausting. Most parents of typical children are able to give verbal instructions less often and the children are able to follow through with the request. The need to be reminded is much, much less. Autistic children have difficulties following directions and need repetitive commands many more times to be able to follow through with what is asked of them. A lot of times, if a situation places the autistic child in an uncomfortable, anxious mood, the child will need more cues and instruction to do what is expected of them. Sometimes the child may just be too distracted to even listen. Of course it is this aspect of continuous disciplining over the same issue that makes it easy for others to judge my parenting skills and makes it easy for others to say my kids are out of control.

The continuous, repetitive commands spoken daily to four autistic children is very challenging. It is sometimes difficult to be patient and analyze the situation because the "children not listening" becomes very frustrating and draining. But "patience is a virtue" is a statement which needs to be followed for the autistic child.

Misconstrued "Authoritative" Evaluations of Negativity

Sometimes a far greater challenge for parents of autistic children is not the children themselves but the individuals that work with their children daily. The parents place an enormous amount of trust and responsibility in the sincere efforts of the professionals who are the autistic child's future. Unfortunately, Dan and I have run into too many professionals who are totally detached from the autistic children they are working with and feel free to make assumptions about the child's future. One therapist found it necessary to tell me Alex would never speak, another told me Mitchell would never write and still another told Dan and I our children had a very poor future ahead. We have had social workers and psychologists ask us why we had more children after Danielle's diagnosis and how could we possibly handle all the sadness we experience every day? Statements, questions and assumptions like these examples deepen the grief and despair for parents of autistic children.

My opinion is if an individual works with a special needs child their heart MUST be involved as well. The professional has to care about the child and all the hope and love the parents hold true in their hearts in order for the professional to truly see the autistic child for who they really are, not placing a "one is just like another" perspective. Unfortunately, parents of autistic children hear more discouraging news than encouraging news on a daily basis. This is one reason why it is so easy to become depressed and lose hope. But as a parent of autistic children my job is not to lose hope but to find it and continue to believe in my children and my ability to be the best mother, supporter and therapist I can be.

The many challenges of autism create a complex life for the parents. There are many different angles to look at when dealing with a situation and all involved with the autistic child should be aware of and compassionate for these many challenges for the parents. Things are not simple nor are they all black and white. Dan and I take one day at a time, one minute at a time, one challenge at a time. We climb each mountain together. The daily tests we face have made us into very strong individuals. I think raising four autistic children is the hardest thing I will ever do in my life. I never thought I was this strong nor did I ever think I could be so weak. This has all made me a strong advocate and I have learned how to fight for what I feel my children need to survive. On the other hand, it has made me into a weak, emotional mother who cries every day tears of joy or despair and hopes the kids do know that everything I do is for them.

ℰℭ

Chapter 11
A Better Understanding for All

As part of my mission of this book is to help parents with autistic children as well as educating emergency personnel, it is also my mission to educate those who come in contact with autistics on a somewhat regular basis.

There is nothing worse than to receive looks of disdain or overhear purposeful ridicule from others when trying to handle an upset autistic child in public. The already overly stressful incident becomes greatly amplified when people treat you like you're an incompetent parent.

Anyone who comes in contact with an autistic child—which includes just about everyone—needs to understand there is a lot going on behind the scenes. I have dealt with so many individuals who simply do not understand what life is like caring for a child that demands so much patience, attention, patience, love and patience... and did I mention patience?

Looks Can Be Deceiving

First, it should be understood that many children with autism show no physical signs like most mentally retarded, those with Down syndrome or someone in a wheelchair. Autistic children look as normal as any uninflected child. Knowing this might hopefully raise the patience level of onlookers when a child happens to throw a fit in a restaurant or other socially condensed environment. A smile towards the parents would be much more productive, and greatly appreciated, than a sneer or a huff. So please think twice before doing the latter. You just might make someone's day by this small, but noble, gesture

After School

I would like to share with school staff and therapists what things are like with an autistic child when he or she is not in the classroom, school or therapy room.

Each of my children deal with the school mornings differently. My Mitchell is six years old and goes to kindergarten. He hates to get up in the morning. He has difficulties with every aspect of independence; he has trouble with sequencing events (as an occupational therapist once put it). He needs cues on how to dress himself with each and every step. When I say every step, I mean every step. "Take off your pajama bottoms, take off your pajama top, take off your underwear, go to the bathroom," etc. So after I drag him out of bed, cue him through taking off his pajamas and putting on his school clothes and shoes, I have to get his school bag ready. He needs several changes of clothes and underwear put in his school bag (he has accidents with going to the bathroom). I write in his communication notebook how he slept and how he did since he got home from school the day before, for example, "Alex was very hyper, tired, etc." I then make him breakfast after I show him three different choices to pick out to eat.

Alex has an outside lock on his door because of his poor safety awareness. He bangs on his door when he is awake. I have a monitor outside his bedroom door to listen to him and a camera inside his room to watch his every move. I know what every sound is. Before I bring him down from his bedroom I have his clothes ready for him to put on. Alex needs to be monitored continuously. He is very impulsive, inpatient and moves fast. Before he leaves for school he will change the movie in the VCR five times and strip off his clothes two times (because he needs to go to the bathroom). I will have to bring him down from upstairs or up from the basement sometimes two to three times. Dan and I are constantly chasing him.

Mitchell is the very opposite of Alex. Mitchell is very independent but he wants everything at once. While he is dressing I have him choose between two things that he may want for breakfast. I then make his breakfast.

Danielle plays in her room when she wakes up. She usually wakes up quite happy. She follows no directions with coming downstairs. I have to hold her hand and guide her down the steps. Once downstairs she does very little to help with dressing. She is very flaccid and has poor muscle tone. I have to lift her limbs to take off and put on her clothes. She hates putting shoes on and will curl her toes or turn her ankles to make this a very difficult task. She also hates to get her hair combed and her teeth brushed. These tasks require a wrestling match every day. Danielle loves breakfast. She loves it so much in fact that she steals her siblings' breakfast if I don't watch her! This can cause major havoc in the morning at times.

Adam requires constant supervision also. He requires me to dress him completely. He will kick and scream while I change his clothes, brush his teeth and wipe him off after he eats. Adam is not potty trained at all and will kick and scream over a diaper change also. This and other behaviors make the mornings very busy. Adam, like Alex, loves to climb. Although Adam can climb just about anything in the house, he is not as agile as Alex and is quite clumsy. He has fallen from the top of the entertainment center, has pulled the television down on himself and he has torn the border from the upper part of his walls around his bedroom as he fell off of his dresser. Adam puts everything in his mouth. He can put a whole matchbox car in his mouth without me seeing any parts of it sticking out. He chews on books, anything paper or cardboard and other plastic toys like Legos, rattles or toy parts. Adam will also eat anything out of the refrigerator, even uncooked meats, sauces and condiments.

I do also write in Danielle's, Alex's and Mitchell's communication notebooks anything the school needs to know.

Dan takes Alex and Danielle to school and brings them home. Mitchell rides on a small school bus, which picks him up and drops him off at the house.

After school, the kids come home in various moods depending on what they did in school that day. This is why communication is so important. Mitchell may come home wiped out and not want to be bothered for a few hours. Dan and I can tell when he is like this. Alex may come home so hyper that it is difficult to calm him down. Danielle may come home very cranky and tantrum about everything. Dan and I never know the disposition of the children until they arrive.

We have learned from much experience what to do in certain situations. For instance, when Mitchell comes home wiped out we use the deep pressure blanket method and leave him alone. Most often after a few hours he is fine and will eat supper. By this time, though, it may be bedtime. So homework is difficult to get done. Alex may come home so hyper that it is difficult to calm him. We try various methods, a snack and a drink, watching a video like Baby Einstein, the deep pressure blanket method or taking him for a walk. A lot of times being outside and doing something physical will calm him. Swimming is great when there's time! Danielle, when she comes home cranky and throwing tantrums over everything usually means she is very tired. We lay her on the couch with a blanket and a movie for some "down time." Sometimes I will read to her or sing some songs. She will usually fall asleep for an hour nap.

Adam is not in school but we can usually tell his mood first thing in the morning and after his nap. Again, little changes make his mood change, and we can be dealing with a screaming, kicking child or a very calm, under-motivated one. Adam likes to scream really loud when things do not go his way. Sometimes he will do this for hours. He also likes to shove others and grab toys and food from them. These behaviors escalate whenever he is in an agitated mood. Any small change in routine causes this behavior. Usually music, a snack or drink, or a spinning toy calms him. If he is too under-motivated (and we cannot get him to eat, drink, get dressed, etc.) Dan and I usually let him be and slowly talk him through what we need him to do.

These are examples of what we do for the children to prepare them for their day, school and when they come home. Of course their moods vary from day to day and so do the techniques we use to help them. School affects how they are when they come home just like home affects their behavior in school. One really affects the other. This is a good example why I cannot stress enough how vital communication is.

I can state from experience that autism is gravely misunderstood by our society from teachers, to social workers, to coaches and parents who don't have an autistic child.

Autistic children should be able to perform just like normal children. If a child wants to take swimming lessons, then he or she should be able to take swimming lessons. The parents should use good common sense when putting their children into activities; and the persons in charge of the activities should trust the parent's ability to know what the autistic child can handle. Typically, people in charge of swimming lessons, baseball, soccer, gymnastics, religious education classes, etc., often have difficulties differentiating between what an autistic child could and should be taught as opposed to how they would treat typical children. So it is important, as a parent, to be involved by letting these individuals know your child's limitations and strong points. For instance, in a religious education class my kids attended, the typical children were expected to memorize prayers, the rosary and definitions of words as well as be able to recite them to the teacher. My children have great difficulties with the memorization of words and abstract concepts. The teacher simply allowed them to read the prayers and definitions from a note card. For swimming lessons, my children had difficulties following the two and three-step directions required for a lot of the swimming movements. They were allowed to simply learn the basics of floating on their backs, swimming to the side of the pool, holding their breath when they went underwater, etc.

Autistic children may not be able to do the same skills as the typical children when they are on a soccer team, a baseball team, in swimming lessons, in gymnastics and so forth, but those in charge should be able to modify their materials to include the autistic child. Of course, this does not mean special treatment, it means meeting the expectations that is right for each child. Every child is different - with or without autism.

These and other misconceptions have been a driving

force behind my writing this book; mainly because misunderstanding autism has lead to improper and unjust dealings with autistic children as a whole. Speaking from experience, my children have been treated, at times, as though they had a plague. For instance, my son, Alex, was kicked off of a sports team for no reason other than the fact that he was labeled with autism. He did not behave any better or worse than the other kids yet the coach said he could not come back.

Needless to say, I protected him from the ignorance by revealing that there were no "rules" whatsoever that warranted this irrational, impulsive and arbitrary action. Alex was ultimately allowed to participate, but only after enduring the degrading experience of banishment while Dan and I suffered the excruciating pain of the fact that someone had mentally harmed our beautiful boy. This was amplified by the fact that it was founded upon a simple lack of understanding of autism. I'm sure that at least one great philosopher or prolific writer had, at one time or another, declared that it is human nature to fear what we don't understand.

This book gives me hope. It sheds some light on this lonesome burden Dan and I feel we face. I pray that it will enlighten those most dear to us—our friends and our families. I hope that it will help our old friends come back to us—those who strayed once they found out about our children.

I don't blame or hate anyone, because I "understand" them. I understand the way they feel. And now I want others to understand me and my husband, and mostly—my children. I also hope, most of all, that this book will help my children lead better lives; that all children with autism be understood and treated fairly and with greater respect for their amazing courage to face each day though they are so much more difficult to confront. With you reading this book,

I know I am doing something, not sitting in effect of it all in hopes that someone else will make things better than they are.

It is hard for me to remember my life before autism. I know it existed but to me it is like a dream. When I think of my life then, I wonder what it was like to feel "normal." This book is a walk through the most private moments of my life. I expose intimate details of my children's struggles and triumphs. I share information that no one else knows except Dan, the children and myself. My wish is that this intimate, valuable information will help my children and other children with autism spectrum disorders by making others understand what it is like to be a parent of these children.

Nothing is easy and nothing is taken for granted. Parents have autism on their minds twenty-four hours a day whereas professionals or individuals who work with or around autism can leave it behind and go home. I am proud of my children and everything they are and can do. I will always wish and pray that I can do more for them. This book is my gift to them. With this book, I hope to make their future and other children with autism spectrum disorders' future mean something. I truly believe these children were brought on this earth to do great things and as long as I am alive, I will keep advocating for my children so that this belief can be established.

When I held each of my babies in my arms for the first time, I vowed to be the best mother I could be. This promise has been more difficult than I could have ever imagined, but nonetheless I will continue to advocate for what is right for them so that they will someday be happy, successful individuals. I love my children from the bottom of my heart, to the depths of my soul and with all the strength I have. This will never change no matter how hard things get. The only thing I hope will change is the way others view autism and autism spectrum disorders. The responsibility for the future of an autistic child does not only lie with the parents. It lies with all who come in contact with an autistic child.

I want to change the way the world looks, thinks, feels and acts towards this topic and the subjects (the individuals and their loved ones) borne with it. Please share what you have now learned with others. One person at a time, we can make a difference in the improving the lives of people with autism and their loved ones by doing so.

ॐ

Chapter 12
What Autism Has Taught Me

An individual is forced to look deeper into oneself and their life when an unexpected tragedy happens. One's inner strength, faith in God and outlook on life is tested. Autism has taught me many things about life and has changed me forever. If there has to be something good that comes from my children's diagnoses, I feel it is the way I look at each day. I would like to share these lessons in this final chapter of my book.

Autism has taught me to notice and praise the smallest, simplest things in life. By appreciating the small things in life I have become a person who takes nothing for granted. I find myself at peace with a sunny day, a hot cup of coffee, a compliment from a stranger and going on a long evening walk. I find a miracle in Mitchell's smile. It warms my heart when Danielle looks into my eyes, even if it is for only a second. It brings tears to my eyes when Alex says "Mom," for hearing him say any word is a joyous occasion. I cherish each time Adam comes to me with open arms for a hug because any response of my presence is very uplifting. My children make small, significant accomplishments each day; with autism there are few great accomplishments. It is these small achievements I look forward to each day.

Autism brings with it many feelings, difficult decisions to be made and a huge amount of challenges each and every day. Raising four autistic children has taught me to forgive my, and other's, mistakes more easily. I am more able to give others a second chance and more understanding when others ask for one. Autism has taught me to give everyone "the benefit of the doubt" and not make a mistake out to being larger than what it is. I think this has made me into a more patient person. As I said before autism requires an enormous amount of patience and understanding. This has carried over to all parts of my life.

Autism has taught me to be thankful. Thankful for everything that I have, the people in my life and the things that happen to me each day. There is a lot of sadness with autism and through the dark gloom, a parent has to be attuned to those joyous moments that bring inner thankfulness. I am thankful each day for those who work with my children: therapists, teachers, TSS workers, behavioral specialists and case managers. I am thankful for my family and friends who do (seemingly) little things to help and who support our family with positive, encouraging statements. It is "the little things" that sometimes mean the most: my mother, grandmother, aunts and uncles who send their prayers and pray for my family; my dad, brother and his family and my sister with her family, who give hugs and kisses to me and my children every time they see us; my neighbors who give the kids birthday and Christmas presents and who come over and baby sit or lend us things when we just can't make it to the store. These are the individuals who make us aware that we are doing just fine. Of course, I am thankful for my children and who they are. I am thankful for the loving, patient, family devoted man I married. I am thankful for every word they utter and every hug they seek. I am thankful for each smile and every academic accomplishment. I will never stop being thankful for all they do and everything in my life.

Autism has taught me to cherish each moment in life, even the difficult times. Unfortunately, my children will only be children for a short time and it is easy to get caught up in the day in, and day out hardships of autism and to let time pass by unnoticed. I have learned to look at Mitchell, Alex, Danielle and Adam as children first, then autism. I have learned to laugh and enjoy the daily chaos of having seven little children. At times when my house is loud and full of activity, I sit back and smile. I know someday my house will be quiet and my children will be more interested in other things and not mom. I also know the future of my autistic children is unknown. Will they go to college? Will they marry? Will they have a career? Will they have children? It is difficult to think of these questions and to think of all the uncertainties. The only questions I can answer are here and now. I look at each day as a new opportunity to enjoy my children and all that this brings.

Autism has taught me to never give up no matter how difficult things seem to be. As mentioned before, the results of constant therapy and schooling do not always appear right away. An autistic child can have what seems to be no progress for months and then the efforts become rewarded. By not seeing an immediate response, it makes it easier for a parent to give up mentally, physically and emotionally. But it is the actual awaited result that makes it worth all the time and effort. Alex has gone to sensory integration therapy for two years now. To see him start writing his name, counting to twenty and talking more makes the therapy worthwhile. I have learned from my children that sometimes things take time and the idea is to not give up. The saying, "Good things are worth waiting for," is very true, but I would also add "so don't give up!"

Autism has taught me to be proud of what my children are able to do. The many professionals that come into my home everyday to analyze and evaluate my children look for the weak areas that need more attention. It is their job to improve these areas by developing strategies and goals. It is easy to get wrapped up in what the children cannot do. I, however, have learned to be proud of what they *can* do. I am proud of Mitchell's ability to read and write over one hundred words, Alex's ability to put anything together better than any grown mechanic, Danielle's love for babies and animals, and Adam's love for music and how ticklish he is when you play with him. I am proud of my children's abilities and I make sure they know it. I have also expressed how proud I am to others when it seems my children's inabilities are more of the focus.

When a parent has a child with autism that parent is involved with many different individuals. Autism has taught me to make no enemies. When dealing with many people, I am always honest about my opinion, determined about what I want and humble about my mistakes. There have been times where I have had advocates or case managers step in on and help with issues that I couldn't get solved. This usually got someone's attention and I was given a chance to speak about my concerns, but I made sure the conversations ended peacefully. Unfortunately, the individuals the parents rely on the most are those that don't always know nor understand about autism fully because they don't live it day in and day out. It can be difficult at times to deal with these people, but it is important not to make any enemies and to provide these individuals with good communication and respect. They may be with the children for a very long time and their involvement may affect the autistic child's future. It is imperative that the parents keep these individuals on a good note and not develop enemies that the autistic child may need to rely on.

Autism has taught me to never lose sight of my dreams even if they are different than what I expected. My dream was to be a wife and mother. I prayed about it every day. I knew this was what I wanted to be in life. This dream steered my decisions to go to college (I had to have a good job if I was going to raise a big family) and who I developed relationships with. This dream of being a mother and wife is what made me into who I am today. Although the thought of being a mother of four autistic children never entered my mind, I have no regrets for seeking and finding my greatest dream. I hope my children have a dream as deep and real as I once had. I hope they are willing to accept that dream even if it is not "perfect." My dream now is to, one day, see my four autistic children holding their high school diplomas with a successful, hopeful future ahead. I have learned to go for my dreams no matter how hard I have to work, and accept the dream no matter what it brings with it.

Autism has taught me to think and speak positively. I now look at life as always having hope and if a bad circumstance arises I look for a positive solution. With autistic children it is easy to look at only the negative because there are so many difficulties to face everyday. When my children were first diagnosed with autism, I had lost hope and confidence in everything I knew. I was lost in my own grief and heartache, but I soon learned that in order for my children to be successful, happy individuals, I had to think positive and look at possibilities and what can happen. My children can become independent, successful individuals. My children can be accepted by other children with some education and efforts on my part and the typical children's part. I keep these positive words in my mind all of the time. These positive words drive me to keep on going and plugging away day after day. The need for a positive outlook has carried over into other parts of my life including my workplace. I get up each morning with the attitude that today is going to be a good day. I focus on the good of each day. By thinking positively, I have helped myself get through some very stressful times, and I better handle difficult situations that may arise. Thinking positive sometimes also means surrounding yourself with positive people. Dan and I have found that it is more healthy for us to socialize and be around individuals who are more positive than it is to be around those who "drag us down". Of course this sometimes cannot be avoided, but because autism brings with it so much heartache and difficulties, it is more healthy to be around those who support the positive outlook than those who like to focus on the negativity in life. Dan and I have made some difficult decisions and some of these decisions have been who we talk to and embrace in our life because of the special circumstances we face each day.

Autism has taught me the true meaning of sadness and disappointment. I had never felt true sadness or disappointment until the day my children were diagnosed with autism. I learned from this experience what others must feel when they go through difficult situations like their child dying, becoming terminally ill or being abducted. I have learned the true meaning of empathy. Anytime someone needs comfort or support I feel compelled to give it. Remembering the day a group of people gave Mitchell, Alex, Danielle and Adam the diagnoses of autism brings tears to my eyes even today. The diagnosis given each time did not get any easier. Going through this emotional experience has taught me to be empathetic to others' feelings, and instead of ignoring their grief, I pray for them or express my concern in person.

Autism has taught me never to judge anyone and to handle situations with an open mind. Unfortunately, people find it necessary to blurt out their opinion even if they do know what they are talking about. Autism brings with it no physical abnormalities most of the time. Therefore when an autistic child expresses difficulties in public or in front of extended family members the child is labeled as misbehaving and the parents as "bad" role models. It is very degrading, and being a parent of an autistic child is very emotionally traumatic, especially when it is family members who simply like to judge instead of learn about autism.

Autism has taught me to never judge anyone. I now look at each situation in my life with an open mind. I think to myself "Well, maybe I don't know the whole situation." If a mother is having a difficult time with her child in a grocery store I pray silently for that mother. I never make judgments or accusing stares. All of us are in this life to work together. The only way this can happen is if we try to understand each other without condemnation and with an open mind.

Autism has taught me to be flexible. My father once told me that the best quality in a husband is "flexibility." I did not understand what he meant until I married a man who was this way. It is vital to be a flexible person when dealing with autism. My children need a structured schedule, of course, but they also need flexible parents who are willing to go with their moods and difficulties when planning activities. For instance, Dan and I may want to go to Pittsburgh to visit my family on a day that Danielle is having a big tantrum day, Alex is very hyper and can't be calmed down, Mitchell is seeking pressure and needs to be under his weighted blanket or Adam is kicking and screaming about everything. Dan and I may then cancel our plans. There have been many times Dan and I haven't gone to family outings and neighborhood picnics due to difficulties with the children. There are days our autistic children just simply cannot tolerate going somewhere, being with a large crowd of people or being with a babysitter. This has carried over into the rest of my life. I have learned to be flexible with my clients at work and their families. I have learned to be more flexible with myself and not get so upset if I can't get my daily goals accomplished.

I never realized how much inner strength I had until I was faced with the uncertainties, difficulties and emotions of autism. I pull from that inner strength every day to get through difficulties I face and things that remind me how different my life really is from others. Sometimes I forget all that I am missing by not having typical children - conversations after school, slumber parties, bedtime prayers, sharing secrets. Sometimes I forget that others are not experiencing the same difficulties with their children as I am with mine like Alex, who is nonverbal, getting out of the house and running across a busy road or Danielle throwing a tantrum for an hour about nothing really specific or Adam putting holes in the walls and screaming for hours on end. It is these times of despair that I pull from my inner strength, hold my head up, think positive, thank God for what I do have and move on.

I feel I have learned more from my autistic children than they will ever know. They have taught me how to be a better person. Autism is a complex condition that affects each child differently. By having four children experiencing autism in four different ways, I have learned many ways of looking at life. I have learned how to be positive, flexible, thankful, happy, proud, empathetic, tolerable, motivated and open-minded. When I got married eight years ago, I never thought my life would be as it is today. I truly feel autism touched my life to make me a stronger person. My hope is that my strength will make my children stronger, motivated individuals willing to face the future with whatever it may bring.

All autistic children are different just like typical children are different. Autistics have their talents and passions just like others. Many have amazed the world with accomplishments of literature and music composition. Others have astounded scientists and mathematicians with abilities to crunch numbers faster than a computer and other hyper-human abilities.

Society has misunderstood autism, and hopefully this book has brought parents, guardians, relatives, teachers, coaches, strangers… to a place where greater understanding, patience and acceptance lies.

ॐ

Biography

Lori May (Wuenschell) Rakieski has taken on the responsibility of educating parents, emergency personnel, social workers and the public, in general, about autism through talks, lectures and this book. Mrs. Rakieski speaks with parents and teachers on a regular basis all to the greater understanding and coping of this ever-growing syndrome. She has a Bachelor of Science degree in Dietetics and nutrition. She has been a dietitian for hospitals and corporations.

In 1996, Lori and Dan married and, between 1997 and 2004, had six children; four who are with autism.

ഔങ

Recommended Reading

An OT and SLP Team Approach - Nancy Kashman and Janet Mora

Childhood Speech, Language and Listening Problems, 2nd Edition - Patricia McAleer

Autsim: A Sensorimotor Approach to Management - Ruth A. Huebner, Ph.D.

The Child with Special Needs: Encouraging Intellectual and Emotional Growth - Sanly I., M.D., Serena Greenspan, Ph.D., Robin Simon Weider (contributor) and Serens Wieder

Learning Disability: Physcial Treatment and Management - Jeanette Rennie

www.ingramcontent.com/pod-product-compliance
Lightning Source LLC
Chambersburg PA
CBHW060853280326
41934CB00007B/1030